Echoes of the Soul

Navigating
the Path of Grief
and Trauma to
Healing

Shauna Judnich

Echoes of the Soul
© 2024 Shauna Judnich/ISBN: 979-8-9901679-0-2
All rights reserved.

IN MEMORY OF THE DAD
THAT RAISED ME

Contents

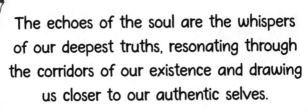

The echoes of the soul are the whispers
of our deepest truths, resonating through
the corridors of our existence and drawing
us closer to our authentic selves.

-SHAUNA JUDNICH

Introduction

Trauma. We've all experienced it, or at least, we will at some point in our lives. Whether it's childhood trauma, abuse, neglect, the loss of a loved one (death, divorce, break-up, end of friendship, etc.), or news of an illness - we won't outrun it, we won't be spared, we will have to face it.

And it is there, when you're staring right at it, not wanting to acknowledge its presence, that you have a choice to make. Let it change you, oftentimes for the worse; let it mold you into something you aren't, allow it to take control of your spirit and your life - OR - let it propel you onto a journey of self-discovery, healing, and a path that quite possibly leads you to your authentic self.

It took me a bit, but I chose the latter when trauma came knocking at my door. It was within the depths of despair that I found a more enlightened path. As I traveled on this path, I started to recognize toxic patterns, relationships, and elements that did not align with my higher well-being. I found that I had remnants of past hurts, emotions, beliefs, and echoes of the soul that lingered in my subconscious, that had molded me into this person who was, and had been, living with guilt, regret, toxic patterns, and a total lack of self-love and worth.

Along the way, I began to write again, I began to create again, I became certified in the healing modalities that helped me most during this journey. I found the only way out of the storm I was in - was to go through. As I continued through, I started assisting others enduring their own phases of grief, trauma, or pain. I discovered a purpose for everything I had uncovered, learned, and created during my journey to healing. I found purpose within the pain. My purpose was to help others, even if in some small way, to navigate towards their path of healing. That is my hope for this book. I hope it brings you peace when you need it, guidance if you're seeking it, support, strength, perspective, and above all - I hope it helps bring you through your own storm.

> "Persevering through hardship is like navigating through a turbulent storm at sea. It's not about being fearless, but about finding the courage to face the crashing waves and relentless downpours. In the midst of the darkest moments, it's important to remember that strength often grows in the struggle."
>
> -SHAUNA JUDNICH

My Story

What a year after death
has taught me

It has been a year to the day this Friday (Oct 28, 2016) since I received the call from my mother that my dad was killed. Killed by a girl who had run a stop sign and hit him while he was out on his brand-new Harley.

I'll never forget that call.

What I remember is my mom saying that the Sheriff had just left, my dad had been killed and me saying, I'm on my way and I hung up. That was the extent of that call. My daughter and I grabbed a few things and headed out.

The next 5 hours (of driving) were a blur.

I remember having to pull over every so often to break down crying, only to pull myself back together so we could get back on the road and get to my parents' house safely. Later we would find out that the girl had been texting and driving and that's why she missed the stop sign and hit my dad. And so began the lessons I would learn....

I learned that for the first 2 months, I would break down all the time, that I would make several more trips back home, for support, for the funeral, the memorial service, to help my mom and later on for the court dates.

During these trips, I learned my dad was loved by so many and had so many wonderful friends, some were new friends, but some were from my very early childhood who lasted the test of time. I learned that anything could trigger the onset of tears. In the beginning, it was stop signs, because every time I had to stop at one, I'd wonder, how could she not have stopped?

I learned that you could wake from a dead sleep, when you finally got to sleep, in tears. Which led into learning about insomnia, something I still struggle with today.

After the first 2 months, I learned about anger. When the District Attorney finally got the case and then informed me (because I called every week to find out the status) that he'd be filing Misdemeanor charges, I traded in my grief for anger and shock. How could someone get a misdemeanor when they blatantly broke the law and killed someone?

I listened to his reasoning, she's a young college student, she has no priors, and it's unlikely a jury would convict a 22-year-old of a Felony, in his experience. I lost it at this point. A misdemeanor!

I called my uncle in a fit of tears and he talked me off the ledge so to speak. I sat back for 2 weeks and tried to come to terms with the fact that this is what was going to happen, that she would get a misdemeanor, probably end up with only probation and that would be the end of that. I needed to let it run its course. That is when I learned about displacing grief. I traded in my grief for my mission. That mission being, getting a Felony charge for the girl who killed my dad.

Although some were not too keen on the idea at first, because if she were to go to a felony trial and the jury were to find her not guilty of a felony, she could walk away with no punishment. A misdemeanor with probation was no different to me than her walking away with nothing.

There were actually two people, one being someone who works for the DA and one being a family member, who told me I "couldn't change the DA's mind, so why was I putting so much energy into it and upsetting myself more," and so I went for it. I did what I do best... research. And along the way, I found a piece of me that had gone missing. The piece that when someone says "you can't" I say...."Watch me."

My Navy JAG Corp training as well as my prior law enforcement background came into play. I found case law, I combed the police report for every single little detail, I made outlines and bullet points and I hounded the District Attorney with phone calls and emails several times a week with all of my research.

Until finally, the day before she was to be arraigned on misdemeanor charges, he changed the charge to a felony (he had actually gotten with his team and went over the case, and some of the things I pointed out, and they determined to charge her with a felony).

For almost 3 months, my life consisted of getting that charge changed. I didn't sleep well, I woke up and got on the computer, I hadn't been to the gym in 4-5 months at this point and I surely was not eating well.

I threw myself into finding justice, and my grief, as well as my life, went by the wayside. I kept thinking that if I could just get the felony charge, I'd feel better. This is when I learned about reality.

The reality was that nothing was going to make it better. This became apparent on the second court date, when she was finally arraigned on the felony charges, and she pleaded not guilty and her and her family walked out of the court-room, with me soon to follow.

I didn't know what I'd do if I saw her when I stepped out of that courtroom and I wasn't prepared for what I did see. I saw her being consoled by her family.

Her... being... consoled.

The girl who lied throughout the police report, who had shown no remorse for what she had done, who had shown no remorse towards my family, not even an apology, not a tearful glance at us, nothing, and she was being consoled?

That's when reality hit. It isn't better - even with the felony charge.

I hugged my family and left immediately and drove the 5 hours home back to the desert. I just couldn't be there anymore because I knew it wasn't better. I had displaced my grief by throwing myself into the case and then reality hit that day.

I sat for 5 days on the couch after that court date.

I sat and watched Prison Break, all four seasons. I lived on Starbucks and Prison Break. It was after those 5 days that I started to try to snap out of it. I needed to get back in the gym, I needed to get back to eating healthy, and I needed to get my life back because my downward spiral was surely affecting my own health and my family. That girl had already taken so much from me, I couldn't let her take the rest of me.

It has been a struggle ever since, trying to get back to who I was and trying to live with who I am now.

There were more court dates that followed, but they were quick continuances and I just couldn't make that 5 hour drive each way for 5 minutes of court because the emotional toll after each 5-minute court date was too much.

The court part of it is still ongoing and there is light at the end of the tunnel as we now have a Preliminary Court date of Nov 9 (2016). I hope that it will all end soon so that there will finally be some sort of closure, at least one chapter closed, if you will.

What I also learned, and this is one of the biggest lessons of all, was that people will be there for you. And some will not understand. Some will not understand that you go through these phases, not just the grief phases, but internal phases as well. There were days, weeks, even months when I didn't really want to talk to anyone, except my immediate daily family.

Friendships went by the wayside, even some family relations, because sometimes you are in a hole, so deep in the hole that you just don't know how to climb out. A hole filled with regret, sorrow, anger and hopelessness. You don't feel social, you don't feel yourself, actually, you really don't feel anything at all.

And that is where the struggle begins.

I've experienced loss before, grandparents, other family, even friends/shipmates while in the military. But when you experience loss at this level, and for me, a loss that was unforeseen, it changes you. Some people will get it, some won't.

I learned that support and love can be shown in many forms. It can be a friend stopping by with a book that helps with grieving and who texts little texts daily to just let you know they are there and they care, whether you respond or not. It is shown in the form of a friend bringing you an ice chest full of water and healthy snacks for a long drive you have to make for an important court date.

Or when your training partner can just look at you when you get to the gym and know that regardless of the journey we are on or our dedication, they say let's forgo the workout and go have breakfast and they are just there, to listen, to share in your grief or just share in the moment.

It can come in the form of posts on your FB, from friends who know the inner strength you do have, even when you've forgotten, and support you by telling you to straighten your crown and take care of business. It can be your best friend who answers the phone every time and just listens, whether it be crying, anger, complaining, or just talking through things.

It can be a text containing "Drive safe" or "where are you" or a frantic call that there's been an accident somewhere near our home and asking if you're ok shows how much someone loves you, considering I get them almost daily from my daughter.

I've learned that your heart can be broken 7 ways to Sunday when your daughter comes down the stairs, crying, because she went to put on a t-shirt and realized it was her grandfather's memorial t-shirt, or you find your sister sitting in the garage at your parents' house, sobbing, or when you and your brother find your dads phone at the crash site the day after it happens.

I learned that others had lost a parent or parents during this time too. One, who was an acquaintance for many years and became a friend. As she had said, "It is a friendship formed through tragedy/grief." And you find comfort in them, because they get it, they are in that same hole, desperately trying to get out, to feel normal.

Although those who lost a parent were all of different circumstances, the pain was the same and I found comfort in talking to them or even to those who had lost someone years before.

I've learned that old friendships can be renewed and that you can almost pick right back up where you left off, even if since childhood and there's an old familiar comforting feeling, because they too knew your dad.

I also learned that death brings misunderstandings. Well, in a case where someone is killed or dies unexpectedly, sometimes you are left with questions that will never have any answers. And assumptions can tear you apart. I learned that things will never be the same and that seeing pictures of my dad pop up on Facebook by family members, still takes my breath away every time.

I've learned that I have changed as a person......

Some for the better, as my driving has definitely improved, whereas before my lead foot always led the way, now I slow down and just enjoy the drive.

Some, not so much for the better.....

As I've found myself pulling away from people and have lost contact with people who did mean something to me because I just can't seem to get off this roller coaster.

I've also learned that you start to re-evaluate things....

Whether that be friends, family, choices, beliefs or your own life's purpose (where you are/what you do etc) for that matter.

Some people dealing with grief will need to express it more than others, it could be daily, or every few months or even a year/s later. They may pull away as they don't recognize themselves or this life they now have. Let them. Let them be who they are at that time and let them come back to you when they feel they can.

I've learned that friends will say that it will get easier or better or that they are praying for you, because they don't know what else to say, I mean really, what can you say? But it doesn't get easier or better, it just gets different.

Life does go on, just in a different way.

Much like the Navy and moving every few years, you have to adapt. Adapt and overcome. I've learned that it is still going to take me some time to reach that point, if ever.

I've learned to have compassion for people I don't even know who have suffered through the same kind of tragedy. One in particular, I have become friends with on Facebook and my heart goes out to her and the pain she is going through as the girl who killed her husband by texting and driving (actually she killed two people that day by texting and driving) was sentenced on a misdemeanor charge. Because of that, I've learned our justice system needs to improve and that laws need to be changed.

I have NOT learned forgiveness though.

My heart is bitter towards that girl. People say it was a mistake made, unintentional, however, to me, it was intentional to text and drive thereby running that stop sign and killing my dad.

And this may eat me up internally and really, it only affects me, but I don't forgive her.

To quote a post I saw on FB by a friend:

> "To forgive is to set a prisoner free and discover that prisoner was you"
> -LEWIS B. SMEDES.

I am still that prisoner; I may always be.

If you take anything from this, I hope that it would be to please not text and drive. Or refrain from any distracted driving or drunk driving. Not only could you prevent injury or death to yourself, but also from taking the life of someone else.

Although that in itself is horrible, taking a life, it's those left behind that have to deal with the emotions and pain for the rest of their lives. They become different people, some possibly for the better, but for many, the difference is a never-ending battle between who they were, who they want to be and who they now are.

And it's a painful daily struggle.

I also hope that you have gained some insight and understanding into what it's like, so that if you're ever on the flip side and a friend or family member is dealing with grief or tragedy, you'll understand that if people pull away, or if they post something daily or if every time you talk to them, their grief comes up, you understand what they are going through and that if they pull away or don't respond or don't call, it's just that they are broken, and trying to put the pieces back together again, only in a different way and it may take a while.

"What a year after death has taught me" was originally a Facebook post I posted after the 1st year of my dad's death that garnered the attention of Thunder Roads Northern California Magazine. They asked if they could print it in their Feb 2019 issue. I wrote for them two other times thereafter with the outcome of the trial and about the dangers of texting and driving.

Grief

> "Just as the ocean waves ebb and flow, grief too has its tides - moments of calm and times of crashing. With time, we learn to navigate these emotional waters and find the strength to sail through the storm."
>
> —SHAUNA JUDNICH

When the trial ended, after 3 years, the girl who killed my dad was convicted of the felony. I walked out of that courtroom and went to a corner and cried, sobbed really. And it wasn't the type of sobbing that would relate to a victory; it was an outpouring of raw emotion. My mother came over to me and said, "What's wrong, you got what you wanted?!"

No, I got what I thought I wanted, what I thought would justify it all, what I thought was justice for my dad. What I was left with was what I didn't have the chance to acknowledge during the 3 years because I was so hell-bent on that conviction and the anger that raged inside of me for 3 years...

GRIEF.

Now that I was facing it, I began to scour the internet for anything that would help make sense of what I was feeling, something that would just make me feel better. It's a lie I told myself over and over, that there was "something" that would change the way I was feeling. And then one day, I came across this response on a Reddit post, and I thought, wow, that explains it exactly.

Reddit user GSnow on Grief:

"Alright, here goes. I'm old. What that means is that I've survived (so far) and a lot of people I've known and loved did not. I've lost friends, best friends, acquaintances, co-workers, grandparents, mom, relatives, teachers, mentors, students, neighbors, and a host of other folks. I have no children, and I can't imagine the pain it must be to lose a child. But here's my two cents. I wish I could say you get used to people dying. I never did. I don't want to. It tears a hole through me whenever somebody I love dies, no matter the circumstances. But I don't want it to "not matter". I don't want it to be something that just passes. My scars are a testament to the love and the relationship that I had for and with that person. And if the scar is deep, so was the love. So be it. Scars are a testament to life. Scars are a testament that I can love deeply and live deeply and be cut, or even gouged, and that I can heal and continue to live and continue to love. And the scar tissue is stronger than the original flesh ever was. Scars are a testament to life. Scars are only ugly to people who can't see. As for grief, you'll find it comes in waves. When the ship is *first wrecked, you're drowning, with wreckage all around you. Everything floating around you reminds you of the beauty and the magnificence of the ship that was, and is no more. And all you can do is float. You find some piece of the wreckage and you hang on for a while. Maybe it's some physical thing. Maybe it's a happy memory or a photograph. Maybe it's a person who is also floating. For a while, all you can do is float. Stay alive. In the beginning, the waves are 100 feet tall and crash over you without mercy. They come 10 seconds apart and don't even give you time to catch your breath. All you can do is hang on and float. After a while, maybe weeks, maybe months, you'll find the waves are still 100 feet tall, but they come further apart. When they come, they still crash all over you and wipe you out. But in between, you can breathe, you can function. You never know what's going to trigger the grief. It might be a song, a picture, a street intersection, the smell of a cup of coffee. It can be just about anything...and the wave comes crashing. But in between waves, there is life. Somewhere down the line, and it's different for everybody, you find that the waves are only 80 feet tall. Or 50 feet tall. And while they still come, they come further apart. You can see them coming. An anniversary, a birthday, or Christmas, or landing at O'Hare. You can see it coming, for the most part, and prepare yourself. And when it washes over you, you know that somehow you will, again, come out the other side. Soaking wet, sputtering, still hanging on to some tiny piece of the wreckage, but you'll come out. Take it from an old guy. The waves never stop coming, and somehow you don't really want them to. But you learn that you'll survive them. And other waves will come. And you'll survive them too. If you're lucky, you'll have lots of scars from lots of love. And lots of shipwrecks."*

I cried all the way through reading this the first time. I cried through it the next 50 times I read it too. Hell, I cried right now writing it.

Although I found many things that helped me through this journey, this has remained one of the most cherished things I have ever found on the internet, or ever read, for that matter. I have shared it at least 100 times with other people in my life that experienced loss, and they've all agreed that the profound advice written in that post was helpful in one way or another.

An odd thing that I did during the grief journey was buy shoes. Like 70-80 pairs in a 4-month period, I shit you not! To some, that may be nothing, but I live in the desert where you can typically find me in flip-flops, hiking shoes, or occasionally, tennis shoes. So, to buy 70-80 pairs of shoes ranging from boots to high heels to wedge sandals was really out of character for me.

All I knew is that it made me happy at the time. To be perfectly honest, I never wore even 1/4 of them; most still had tags on them years later when I was finally able to reflect and let go, so I donated more than half of them.

This, I found out later, is called comfort shopping or grief splurges. Which is okay to do, in moderation. It becomes a problem when you start racking up credit card bills that you aren't able to afford, which in turn brings on a whole host of other problems - anxiety, regret, buyer's remorse, all things that you really don't need to add on top of what you're already feeling.

I was chasing that "feel-good" feeling - dopamine. It's similar to those who turn to alcohol or comfort food, most times in excess, during grief. Mine was shoes.

With what I learned about this, I created a list of things to consider if comfort shopping, for any reason, finds its way into your life:

- **Financial Impact:** Evaluate your budget and financial situation. Comfort shopping can lead to overspending and financial strain if not kept in check.

- **Emotional Awareness:** Reflect on your emotions and the reasons behind your desire to comfort shop. Are you seeking relief from stress, boredom, or other emotional issues? Understanding your emotions can help you address the root cause.

- **Alternative Coping Strategies:** Explore alternative ways to cope with stress or emotions that don't involve shopping. This could include activities like exercise, meditation, talking to a friend, or engaging in a hobby.

- **Mindful Spending**: Practice mindful spending by being aware of your purchases and their impact on your overall well-being. Consider whether the items you're buying genuinely contribute to your happiness or if they provide only temporary relief.

- **Delayed Gratification:** Try implementing a "cooling-off" period before making non-essential purchases. Give yourself time to reconsider and decide if the item is something you genuinely need or if it's a result of impulsive emotional spending.

- **Setting Limits:** Establish limits on your spending. Set a budget for non-essential purchases and stick to it. Having clear boundaries helps prevent impulsive and excessive spending.

- **Quality Over Quantity:** Focus on the quality and value of the items you buy rather than the quantity. Consider investing in meaningful and lasting purchases rather than accumulating a large number of items.

- **Social Support:** Talk to friends, family, or a mental health professional about your emotions and coping mechanisms. Having a support system can provide alternative perspectives and assistance in finding healthier coping strategies.

- **Self-Reflection:** Regularly reflect on your shopping habits and assess whether they align with your values and long-term goals. Consider whether comfort shopping is a temporary coping mechanism or a habit that needs adjustment.

- **Seeking Professional Help:** If comfort shopping becomes a persistent issue and negatively impacts your life, consider seeking help from a mental health professional who can provide guidance and support in developing healthier coping strategies.

As I mentioned before, some people will turn to alcohol or food during grief. Although I didn't necessarily turn to either of those in excess, I did start drinking coffee in excess. You might think, what's the big deal, it's just coffee. It wasn't just coffee; it was hot peppermint mochas from a well known coffee place, and it wasn't just one a day.

I began going to this certain coffee place that was close to my house, and really, besides the shoe shopping, that was the extent of me getting out of the house. Sometimes I went two to three times a day. Again, I was chasing that dopamine, and hot peppermint mochas were my fix. With whipped cream.

Within a couple of weeks, one of the baristas, Dylan, could tell my voice over the order speaker and would say, "Hi, Shauna," when I ordered, if he was on duty. He also began to notice my demeanor at the drive-thru window; most times I had just rolled out of bed (or off the couch), hair tousled, face unwashed, and tear-stained.

He asked one day if I was okay, and I just let it all out. My dad had been killed, the trial, and I was having a hard time. Dylan was sympathetic and compassionate. Not just that time, but every time. Oftentimes thereafter, he would even buy my drink for me. I found out later that he and my daughter had gone to high school together, and he and I forged a friendship, as well as he introduced me to his parents, who I also became friends with.

I mention this story about Dylan because when you are in a state of profound hopelessness, sometimes there are moments when a light shines, a glimmer, and Dylan, along with the hot peppermint mochas, were my first glimmers. Kindness, compassion, and just acknowledgment in general go a long way. So does whipped cream on top of a mocha, I'm just saying. For someone that you see on occasion, and for me, just through a drive-thru, to notice something completely off about you speaks volumes to the fact that there **ARE** good people out there.

The point about the excess coffee is that because I was drinking this sugary drink 1-3 times a day, practically every day, for a few months and really not eating much, I packed on 30 lbs in a short amount of time. Okay, it was 50.

Which led to me feeling like shit, in general, about myself, as well as it tore up my stomach because I was barely eating much and it was mostly carbs if I did eat. I was a hot mess. Which was an added stressor I really didn't need at that time.

My lack of food, or at least, good food when I did eat, and my mocha addiction, I later discovered, was a form of disordered eating behavior (emotional eating) due to grief. Emotional eating due to grief refers to the behavior of using food as a way to cope with and manage intense emotions associated with the loss of a loved one or other significant sources of grief or trauma. When individuals experience grief, they may turn to eating as a means of seeking comfort, distraction, or emotional relief.

This type of eating behavior is often driven by emotional factors rather than physical hunger. People may find temporary solace or distraction from their emotional pain by consuming certain foods. This can lead to overeating, making unhealthy food choices, or engaging in patterns of eating that are not based on nutritional needs but rather on emotional needs.

It's important to note that emotional eating during grief is a common response, and people may use it as a way to self-soothe during a challenging time. However, when this behavior becomes a predominant coping mechanism and negatively impacts overall well-being, seeking support from friends, family, or mental health professionals can be beneficial.

If you find yourself emotionally eating during grief, here are some tips that may help:

- **Self-Awareness:** Pay attention to your emotions and identify triggers that lead to emotional eating.

Understanding your feelings can help you address the root cause.

- **Seek Support:** Share your feelings with friends, family, or a therapist. Having a support system can provide comfort and help you process grief in a healthier way.

- **Mindful Eating:** Practice mindful eating by being present during meals. Pay attention to the taste, texture, and smell of your food. This can help you become more aware of your eating habits.

- **Find Alternative Coping Mechanisms:** Explore alternative ways to cope with grief, such as journaling, art, exercise, or meditation. Engaging in activities that bring you comfort without involving food can be beneficial.

- **Establish Routine:** Create a routine for meals and snacks. Having regular eating times can help prevent impulsive emotional eating episodes.

- **Keep Healthy Snacks Available:** Stock up on nutritious snacks so that if you feel the urge to eat, you have healthier options readily available.

- **Stay Hydrated:** Drink plenty of water throughout the day. Sometimes, dehydration can be mistaken for hunger.

- **Avoid Restrictive Diets:** Avoid strict or restrictive diets during the grieving process. Allow yourself to eat a balanced diet that includes a variety of foods.

- **Physical Activity:** Incorporate regular physical activity into your routine. Exercise can help improve mood and provide a healthy outlet for emotions.

- **Professional Help:** If emotional eating becomes a significant challenge, consider seeking support from a mental health professional who can offer guidance and coping strategies.

Remember, coping with grief is a personal journey, and it's okay to seek help when needed. If you have concerns about your emotional eating habits, consulting with a healthcare professional or therapist can provide personalized assistance.

Side note: I currently still drink coffee, but I found a way to enjoy it without packing on the calories or the pounds. I have a much healthier version - cold brew, oat milk and stevia.

PSYCHICS AND MEDIUMS

The next stop on my grief journey was psychics and mediums. I was looking for answers, only, I didn't really know what the questions were. I felt someone had to have the insight I was looking for, hopefully it was those that could channel the departed.

One particular time, I had read that a medium would be having a group session at a local facility not too far from where I live. I couldn't find anyone to attend with me, so I decided to go by myself. Big mistake. As I sat there, in a decent-size group of strangers waiting for the medium to come out, I felt an unusual sense of anxiety, which is not something I typically ever feel. I wanted so badly for my dad to come through. I didn't have a clear thought as to what I wanted from him; I just felt this insistent need for him to come through.

And at that moment, sitting in a chair by myself, surrounded by at least 75 strangers, I began to cry. It was an overwhelming sensation. I couldn't quite pinpoint the reason, but I felt a heavy pressure in my chest. I needed this medium to connect with my dad, and I needed to have a message. But it didn't happen.

As I sat there for the 2 hours this session went on for, watching all these other people get messages and love from "beyond," I became more and more disappointed and, honestly, pretty fucking angry. All of a sudden, I had questions- Why didn't he come through? Doesn't he know I need to hear from him? Doesn't he know I'm struggling? Why not me? Which again, is odd for me because I'm typically "a happy for any and everyone else type of person" but we aren't ourselves during grief, and sometimes, we never really fully return to who we were.

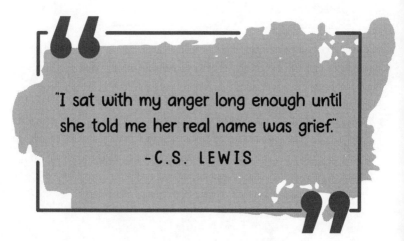

"I sat with my anger long enough until she told me her real name was grief."

-C.S. LEWIS

I sat in my car in the parking lot when it was over and cried for about a good half hour. What I initially thought was going to help me find some solace had actually made things worse for that particular day. My expectations were too high, and I hadn't prepared emotionally at all before heading down this path.

I didn't give up though. I chased this path of various psychics and mediums for a good 6 months after that. I went to private sessions, and some of them actually provided a little of the solace I was looking for. A few even conveyed remarkable messages, referencing details they couldn't have known unless they were intimately familiar with my life, or so I like to believe.

All in all, the psychics and mediums provided a little relief in my grief journey as well as the realization of what my questions actually were. From this experience, I have compiled a list of considerations for those who may travel on a similar path in their journey:

- **Seeking Comfort and Closure:** The primary motivation for visiting a medium is often the desire for comfort and closure. Many individuals hope to receive messages from their departed loved ones or gain insights that can help them cope with grief.

- **Personal Beliefs:** Your beliefs play a significant role in deciding whether to consult a medium. If you hold spiritual or religious beliefs that involve an afterlife or communication with spirits, you may find the idea of visiting a medium more aligned with your worldview.

- **Open-mindedness:** It's important to approach the experience with an open mind. Whether you are a skeptic or a believer, being receptive to the possibility of the unknown can enhance the experience.

- **Understanding the Process:** Before scheduling a session with a medium, it can be helpful to research and understand their methods and practices. Different mediums may use various techniques, such as channeling, psychic abilities, or communication through symbols.

- **Emotional Preparedness:** Keep in mind that the experience may evoke strong emotions. Be emotionally prepared for any messages or information that may come through. It's okay to express feelings of grief, joy, or relief during the session.

- **Ethical Considerations:** Ensure that you choose a reputable and ethical medium. Seek recommendations, read reviews, and verify the medium's credentials before scheduling a session. Ethical mediums prioritize the well-being of their clients and approach their work with sensitivity.

- **Managing Expectations:** While some individuals report profound and meaningful experiences with mediums, others may not receive the specific messages they hoped for. It's essential to manage expectations and recognize that the outcome can vary.

- **Integration with Grief Counseling:** Consider integrating medium sessions with traditional grief counseling. Grief counseling can provide additional support and help you navigate the emotional aspects of loss in a more comprehensive manner.

- **Personal Growth:** Some individuals find that connecting with a medium facilitates personal growth and spiritual development. It can be an opportunity to explore one's beliefs about life, death, and the nature of existence.

- **Respecting Differences:** Understand that people have diverse beliefs and coping mechanisms when it comes to grief. Respect the choices of others, whether they choose to visit a medium or pursue alternative methods of healing.

Ultimately, the decision to visit a medium is deeply personal and varies from person to person. It's essential to approach such experiences with an open heart, maintaining a healthy balance between spiritual exploration and grounded self-care during the grieving process.

INSOMNIA

I grew up in a fairly strict household. And by fairly strict, I mean I was grounded most of my freshman year and read a whole set of Encyclopedia Britannica because of it. Writing that right now made me laugh because half of you will probably have to look up on the internet what an Encyclopedia even is.

Encyclopedia Britannica is a general encyclopedia that consists of 32 volumes. It is a comprehensive reference work that covers a wide range of subjects, including science, history, art, literature, and more. It was our "internet" in the 80s, but not in a cool way. I laugh now also because my husband and kids used to ask at various times why I knew so much "useless" knowledge. Well… I was grounded a lot and I read encyclopedias.

So, what does that have to do with anything? I'm just painting a picture. Although I was grounded a lot, it was typically for my grades, because I hated school, yet I'm actually quite intelligent. And also, for the occasional sneaking out.

The point is, that's the worst I did. Okay, I drank alcohol a couple of times, but that's it. I never tried marijuana (or drugs). For one, I didn't like being grounded for what I thought were "piddly" things, so I sure as hell didn't want to be grounded for life for doing drugs.

Plus, to be totally transparent, I was too chicken shit. This is your brain, this is your brain on drugs, and all. You'll probably have to look that up, too. I swear, the 80s were the greatest! Shortly after high school, I was in the military for 10 years and the police department after that, so trying any type of drugs just wasn't in the cards for me.

So there I was at 47, with another effect of grief - Insomnia. I had it off and on through the trial years and then it just seemed to linger. An acquaintance of mine owned a juice shop, and by juice, I do mean pressed juice, you know, veggies and fruit. However, she was also well-versed in all things THC. I sought her guidance on what might help me get some sleep, and she said to try cannabis oil. So I thought, what the hell, I'm desperate, let's do this!

I went to the dispensary, told them what I needed, and headed home with a vial of pure cannabis oil. No big deal. I started following the directions my friend gave me - put a toothpick tip-size on a little piece of bread about an hour or so before you want to go to sleep. Do that for a week, and then the next week, add an ever so slightly larger amount, and so on and so forth for the following weeks until you build up your tolerance.

I did this the first week and OMG - Best. Sleep. Ever. I thought, why hadn't I done this before?!

Second and third week, I had increased ever so slightly, and I was doing great! I was even waking up anywhere between 5:30-6 am feeling refreshed and ready to go. Waking that early was way out of the ordinary for me, let alone feeling amazing.

Then came the middle of the 4th week. This one night, the oil on the toothpick kind of dribbled a little extra. I figured, oh well, my tolerance is surely built up by now. Wrong! I was SO wrong. About 20-30 mins after I took it, my husband and I went into the garage to smoke a cigarette, and that's when all hell broke loose. Here's how it went:

Me, standing frozen in one spot: "Um, I need some help."

Hubs: "What's wrong?"

Me: "I can't move."

Hubs: "What? Why not?"

Me, almost in tears: "I don't fucking know but I can't."

Hubs: "Ok, ok, I'll help you."

So he stands in front of me with his back to me, and I some-how pick my arms up enough to wrap around his neck, and he kind of drags me into the house. He takes me into our bedroom and helps me lay down.

Me: "I think I need to go to the hospital."

Hubs: "Why?"

Me: "Pretty sure I'm having a stroke, maybe a heart attack. I'm not sure, but I'm starting to go numb around my neck and arm. I think you better call an ambulance."

Hubs: "I don't think that's what's happening."

Me: "Well, it's happening to me, and that's what's happening, so can you call?"

Hubs: "It isn't what's happening. You're high."

Me: "Ok then, well, can you call them? I need to go to the hospital."

Hubs: "What are they going to do there?"

Me: "Give me an IV and flush this shit out, duh!"

Hubs, laughing, mind you: "It doesn't work that way. You're high; you need to sleep it off."

He gets in bed and starts to roll over, giggling. Asshole.

Hubs: "Just go to sleep; you'll be fine in the morning, I promise."

Me: "Ok, but if I die, just remember I was right!"

Hubs: "Oh my God, ok, I'll remember!" (again, laughing)

He rolls completely over, and within minutes, well, he's asleep. I'm left lying there, half numb, leg shaking, waiting for my heart to explode when I have an epiphany - my Fitbit is right there on my nightstand.

I'll put it on, see that my heart rate is clearly close to 200 or whatever death is and I'll wake his ass up and show him I'm right! Got it, strapped it on and….. it's 62.

What. The. Fuck.

Needless to say, I didn't wake up my hubs, nor did I die, and I also never tried any type of marijuana (or drugs for that matter) again. Whether it was the almost 4 weeks of using the oil or just the pure fright of thinking that was my only option, my insomnia cleared up. Nowadays, if I'm up until 2 or 3 am, it's because I had a coffee late in the day or night.

I tell you this story not to make light of grief or to promote drugs (not that I'm judging because I am so a "you do you, boo" type of girl) or even to fill pages. I share this story to illustrate one of the effects of grief I experienced and the steps I took to try to cope. Additionally, I share this story because I wanted to show you another glimmer in the midst of sorrow. Although my husband was right (insert eye roll here), we did have a huge laugh (a rarity for me at that time) the next day when I woke up feeling incredibly refreshed - and alive. There are glimmers of light that start to shine through the dark.

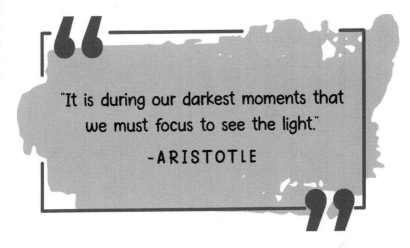

"It is during our darkest moments that we must focus to see the light."

-ARISTOTLE

Insomnia during grief is a common and challenging experience for many individuals. The process of grieving can significantly impact sleep patterns, leading to difficulties falling asleep, staying asleep, or experiencing restorative sleep. Several factors contribute to insomnia during grief:

- **Emotional Turmoil:** Grief brings a range of intense emotions such as sadness, anxiety, and despair.

These emotions can be overwhelming, making it difficult for individuals to relax and fall asleep.

- **Thoughts and Rumination:** Grieving individuals often experience intrusive thoughts and rumination about the loss. These persistent thoughts can disrupt the mind's ability to quiet down, hindering the onset of sleep.

- **Physical Discomfort:** Grief can manifest physically, with symptoms like tension, headaches, and aches. These physical discomforts can make it challenging to find a comfortable sleeping position.

- **Changes in Routine:** Grieving may lead to changes in daily routines and lifestyle, affecting sleep patterns. Irregular sleep schedules and disrupted routines can contribute to insomnia.

- **Nightmares and Disturbing Dreams:** Grieving individuals may experience nightmares or distressing dreams related to the loss, causing them to wake up frequently during the night.

Tips for Managing Insomnia During Grief:

- **Establish a Routine:** Stick to a consistent sleep schedule by going to bed and waking up at the same time each day.

- **Create a Relaxing Bedtime Routine:** Develop a calming pre-sleep routine to signal to your body that it's time to wind down. This may include activities like reading, listening to soothing music, or practicing relaxation techniques.

- **Limit Stimulants:** Reduce or eliminate the intake of caffeine and nicotine, especially in the hours leading up to bedtime.

- **Create a Comfortable Sleep Environment:** Ensure that your bedroom is conducive to sleep—dark, quiet, and at a comfortable temperature.

- **Seek Support:** Talk to a mental health professional or join a support group to address the emotional aspects of grief, which may, in turn, positively impact sleep.

- **Exercise Regularly:** Engage in regular physical activity, but avoid strenuous exercise close to bedtime.

- **Limit Screen Time:** Reduce exposure to screens (phones, tablets, computers) before bedtime, as the blue light emitted can interfere with the production of the sleep hormone melatonin.

If insomnia persists or worsens, it's crucial to consult with a healthcare professional for personalized guidance and support. They can help explore potential underlying issues and recommend appropriate interventions.

Now, should you find yourself experimenting with any form of THC on your healing journey, it's important to note that the use of it or any substance to cope with grief or insomnia is a personal choice, and its effectiveness and appropriateness can vary from person to person. It's important to approach it with caution and consult with a healthcare professional. Here are combined tips that take into account both scenarios:

- **Consult with a Healthcare Professional:** Before using THC for insomnia or grief, talk to your healthcare provider. They can provide personalized advice based on your health history and any potential interactions with medications you may be taking.

- **Start with Low Doses:** If approved by your healthcare provider, start with a low dose and gradually increase it if needed. This helps gauge your tolerance and minimize potential side effects.

- **Consider the Strain:** Different strains of cannabis may have different effects. Some strains are known for their calming and sedative properties, which may be more suitable for both insomnia and managing grief-related symptoms.

- **Timing is Key:** Consider the timing of your THC use. Using it too close to bedtime might interfere with your sleep cycle, while using it during the day may help manage grief-related symptoms. Experiment with different timings to find what works best for you.

- **Be Mindful of Side Effects:** THC can have side effects, including drowsiness, impaired coordination, and memory issues. Be aware of these effects, especially when using THC close to bedtime or during activities that require focus.

- **Create a Relaxing Environment:** Combine THC use with other good sleep practices. Create a calming bedtime routine for insomnia and ensure a supportive environment for processing grief-related emotions.

- **Pain and Discomfort Relief:** For those experiencing physical discomfort associated with grief, THC's analgesic properties may provide relief. However, it's crucial to address the root causes of pain and not solely rely on THC.

- **Emotional Regulation:** THC's mood-altering effects may assist with emotional regulation, providing temporary relaxation or euphoria. It could be considered for managing intense emotions associated with grief.

- **Sleep Aid and Distraction:** THC's sedative effects may help improve sleep quality for insomnia, and its ability to induce relaxation may act as a distraction from overwhelming grief-related emotions.

- **Social Support:** In some cases, using THC may be a social activity, providing a way for individuals to connect with others who share similar experiences of insomnia or grief. However, it's essential to prioritize professional support and counseling.

Remember, these tips are not a substitute for professional medical advice. Always consult with a healthcare professional before incorporating THC or any cannabis product into your routine, especially when dealing with insomnia or grief.

"In the depths of darkness, a glimmer
of hope always shines through,
you just have to recognize it."

—SHAUNA JUDNICH

I've referred to "glimmers" a few times now, and I feel compelled to elaborate about their significance. Looking back, I realize how crucial it is to recognize and embrace these moments, even within the depths of grief. They serve as beacons of hope, small yet powerful reminders that light still exists within the darkness. Reflecting on my own journey, I wish I had been more attentive to these "glimmers" earlier on.

In the context of grief, "glimmers" refer to moments of relief, comfort, or positive experiences during the challenging and often painful process of mourning. These moments can provide a temporary break from the intense emotions associated with grief. Glimmers do not necessarily eliminate grief, but they offer brief glimpses of light during a dark time. Here are some examples of glimmers during grief:

- **Shared Memories:** Recalling and sharing positive memories of the person who has passed away can bring a sense of warmth and connection. It allows individuals to focus on the joyful moments they shared with their loved one.

- **Supportive Friends and Family:** Receiving understanding, empathy, and support from friends and family members can provide comfort during the grieving process. Feeling loved and supported can be a glimmer of light in the midst of sorrow.

- **Nature and Solitude:** Finding solace in nature, whether it's a serene landscape or a quiet garden, can offer moments of peace and reflection. Nature has a calming effect and can provide a temporary escape from the intensity of grief.

- **Acts of Kindness:** Experiencing or witnessing acts of kindness from others can be uplifting. Small gestures, such as a compassionate word or a helping hand, can create moments of connection and comfort.

- **Art and Creativity:** Engaging in creative activities, such as painting, writing, or playing music, can be therapeutic. The act of self-expression can serve as a glimmer by allowing individuals to channel their emotions and find moments of release.

- **Spiritual or Religious Practices:** For those with spiritual or religious beliefs, engaging in rituals, prayer, or attending ceremonies can provide a sense of peace and connection to something larger than oneself.

- **Personal Achievements:** Accomplishing personal goals or milestones, no matter how small, can bring a sense of pride and achievement. It could be as simple as getting out of bed, taking a walk, or completing a daily task.

- **Laughter and Humor:** Sharing a laugh or finding moments of humor, even in the midst of grief, can be a powerful glimmer. Laughter has a healing effect and can temporarily lift the weight of sorrow.

It's important to recognize that grief is a highly individual and complex process, and what serves as a glimmer for one person may be different for another. These moments of light can provide some relief, but they don't replace the need for the grieving process and the range of emotions that come with it.

Healing

> "Healing is a journey of growth and release, shedding - misconceptions, old beliefs, expectations - while embracing your authentic self with compassion and an open mind."
>
> —SHAUNA JUDNICH

I grew up in a family that was Catholic, not that we went to church on a regular basis or anything, but my whole family is Catholic with some of them very devout. During my junior year of high school, I lived with a family who were Christians and who attended church every Sunday. And so, I attended church every Sunday. It never resonated with me. I thought maybe I was just too attention deficit or something to really grasp religion. Nevertheless, throughout my 20s, 30s, and into my 40s, I never connected with any sort of religion.

As I embarked on the healing phase of my personal journey, a profound sense of enlightenment enveloped me, shedding light on aspects that had long eluded comprehension within traditional religious frameworks. It's crucial to note that I don't identify as an atheist, nor do I harbor any animosity towards religion. What I mean is that conventional religious practices never quite resonated with me. It's not that I dismissed the notion of a higher power, a creator, or God – I acknowledged that possibility. However, the structured nature of mainstream religious beliefs failed to instill in me the same unwavering faith that more devout individuals experienced.

My friend, Lorrie, has consistently been a pillar of perspective, supporting my emotions, goals, and overall well-being from the start of our friendship, as well as through my grief and healing journey. She recommended that I have a session with her "energy healer," during my journey, emphasizing the transformative impact it had on her thus far. She shared that she was able to release trapped emotions and the profound revelations she experienced during these sessions. Although intrigued, I found myself oddly skeptical, which is ironic since I went down the path of chasing psychics and mediums.

When I agreed to try out the sessions, I made it clear to Lorrie that I hoped the energy healer wouldn't simply rely on my Facebook story for insights—that would be like taking a shortcut. Lorrie, aware of my analytical mind, laughed at my concern, told me no one would be looking into my Facebook and told me to just sign up.

So, I did.

That was a pivotal moment in my healing journey. Right from the initial session, a transformative process unfolded, serving as an accelerant that propelled me onto numerous paths, leading to profound realizations and guiding me towards a newfound sense of spirituality and purpose.

Let me tell you about Gail and how she would change my life and help me climb out of the darkest hole I had ever been in. Or so I thought. Unbeknownst to me, I had been in quite a hole long before grief knocked at my door.

In my initial session and the subsequent ones with Gail, we conducted them over the phone. Maintaining my level of skepticism, I refrained from sharing any personal information with her in the beginning. Consequently, she had limited knowledge about me, a detail that proved irrelevant in her style of healing sessions, which primarily focus on energy, emotions, and the subconscious mind.

These sessions are known as The Emotion Code and Body Code which are holistic approaches to health and well-being developed by Dr. Bradley Nelson.

During that first session, Gail explained that what she would be doing is releasing trapped emotions and also working on imbalances within the body using the following technique:

Emotion Code:

- **Focus:** Identifying and releasing trapped emotions—negative emotional energies that may become lodged in the body during stressful or emotional experiences.

- **Method:** Practitioners use muscle testing or other forms of energy testing to pinpoint trapped emotions and release them. The release is often done through techniques like using magnets or intention.

- **Purpose:** By releasing trapped emotions, the goal is to restore balance to the body's energy field and address physical and emotional issues that may be associated with these imbalances.

Body Code:

- **Expansion:** The Body Code builds on the Emotion Code by addressing a broader range of imbalances in the body's energy system.

- **Categories:** It identifies and addresses imbalances in six main categories—emotional, energetic, toxicity, circuitry, pathogens, and structural.

- **Techniques:** Similar to the Emotion Code, practitioners use muscle testing or other energy testing methods to identify imbalances. Techniques such as magnets or intention may be employed to clear or rebalance the body's energy.

- **Purpose:** The Body Code aims to promote overall well-being by addressing a wider range of factors that may contribute to health issues, including emotional, energetic, and structural imbalances.

I thought, well, this is a unique approach, but I'm willing to give it a chance—just as long as she doesn't immediately delve into the topic of grief, making me feel like she already knew my story. My skepticism was still out of control.

We spent approximately an hour and a half on the phone, and I was astonished by the session's conclusion. To my surprise, she didn't touch on the subject of grief at all. Instead, she brought up specific emotions tied to certain ages, which struck a chord with me because they related to things that no one could have known.

I'm not going to go through all my sessions, as I worked with her on and off over a 4-year period. However, I do want to emphasize some noteworthy moments from our work together, including the recommendations she provided, the transformative changes I underwent, and how this period truly marked a pivotal shift in progressing with my healing—both from grief and aspects of the past that I believed I had already let go of.

Prior to me starting these sessions, I had a persistent pain on the right side under my rib cage, for like 7 months. Seeking answers, I underwent a battery of tests and scans at the VA to identify the source of the discomfort, exploring possibilities related to the liver, gallbladder, or other factors. Despite exhaustive examinations, no abnormalities were detected, and all my tests indicated excellent health. I just lived with this pain on my side.

Approximately two months into my sessions with Gail, I realized that the persistent pain had vanished. I hadn't made any significant lifestyle changes, hadn't altered my diet, or modified supplements—nothing at all. Curious about this sudden relief, I shared with Gail the history of the pain on my right-side spanning seven months. We revisited the releases we had worked on, and a significant portion centered around anger, spanning various ages and particularly during the trial years. Gail shared with me a chart that illustrated where different emotions manifest and/or correlate in the body. Guess where anger resides.

Yep, you guessed it, in the liver and gallbladder area. I never did have that pain again.

In the initial year of sessions, I was deeply immersed in my journey of grief. Initially, I scheduled sessions weekly (reducing frequency over time), and with each passing session, my skepticism dissipated as revelations began to unfold.

Certain emotions are universal and may be experienced by everyone at various times or ages. However, there are also emotions that might not naturally arise. Take terror, for example, which typically wouldn't manifest at the ages of 18 and 19 unless prompted by specific events. In my case, I had been in an abusive relationship, and terror accurately described some of my experiences.

Session after session, I was filled with amazement at the emotions that surfaced, their resonance, but more importantly, the transformative effect I felt after each release.

It seemed as if a burden was lifting, a veil parting, and a light was illuminating my path. I experienced a newfound lightness, heightened clarity, and a sense of spaciousness for healing, both emotionally and physically. Recognizing my own flaws and toxic patterns, I took steps to address and correct them. I became aware of the weight of regret, guilt, shame, and a lack of self-love or worth that I had carried for a significant portion of my life, contributing to my lower vibrational state.

Upon reflection, I recognized my tendencies during my late teens, 20s, and even into my 30s—making unwise decisions, enduring mistreatment, exhibiting poor behavior towards others, fostering toxic relationships and friendships, and dwelling more in the past than in the present.

I wasn't a total asshole, mind you, and most often, people thought I was a pretty nice, cheerful, and all-around great person. Yet, unbeknownst to me back then, internally, I was a bit fractured. This internal struggle led me to make decisions that I wouldn't even consider today. The brokenness stemmed from events that occurred well before my dad's passing, and the process of releasing trapped emotions made me confront this reality. Gradually, I learned to forgive myself for the coping mechanisms I had adopted during challenging periods in my life as well as during my grief journey.

Inspired by the transformative sessions with Gail and the profound insights gained, I made the decision to pursue certification as a practitioner for both the Emotion Code and Body Code in 2022 and 2023.

My motivation was to assist other family members still grappling with the loss of my dad, aid our rescue dog in overcoming past abuse, and later extend support to veterans. While my efforts have been on a modest scale, I've also had the privilege of assisting friends and additional family members along the way.

Those I've helped along the way have consistently expressed a sense of relief, feeling as if a burden has been lifted or experiencing a newfound lightness. I genuinely believe that this practice creates space for healing within the mind, body, and soul.

Engaging in this work has not only provided me with a sense of purpose, one not driven by accolades or monetary gains, but rather a purpose rooted in assisting those who may be navigating through loss, trauma, or any other challenges. My goal is to help them find their own path of enlightenment and healing.

If you find yourself wanting to try Emotion/Body Code sessions during your healing journey, here are some steps you can take:

- **Find a Certified Emotion Code Practitioner:** Look for practitioners who are certified in the Emotion Code technique. You can search online directories, the official Emotion Code website, or ask for recommendations from friends or online communities.

- **Contact the Practitioner:** Reach out to the practitioner of your choice to inquire about their availability and schedule. Many practitioners offer sessions in person, over the phone, or through online platforms.

- **Ask Questions:** Before scheduling a session, feel free to ask the practitioner about their experience, training, and any specific questions you may have about the Emotion Code process. This can help you feel more comfortable and informed about what to expect.

- **Schedule the Session:** Once you've chosen a practitioner and are satisfied with the information provided, schedule a session at a time that works for both of you.

- **Prepare for the Session:** It can be helpful to prepare for the session by reflecting on any specific issues or concerns you'd like to address. However, it's not necessary to disclose personal details if you're not comfortable doing so.

- **Participate in the Session:** During the session, the practitioner may use muscle testing or other energy testing methods to identify trapped emotions. They will then work on releasing these trapped emotions to restore balance to your energy field.

- **Follow-Up, if Needed:** Depending on your experience, you may choose to have follow-up sessions. Some individuals find that multiple sessions can be beneficial for addressing a range of emotional and physical concerns.

- **Feedback and Communication:** After the session, share any feedback with the practitioner and communicate openly about your experience. This can help the practitioner tailor future sessions to your needs.

Remember that the Emotion Code is considered an alternative or complementary therapy, and individual experiences may vary. If you have any existing medical or psychological conditions, it's advisable to consult with your healthcare provider before exploring alternative therapies.

I'd like to mention that you can locate Dr. Bradley Nelson's book, "The Emotion Code," on Amazon. I personally explored it before enrolling in courses and obtaining certification. This initial engagement allowed me to work on myself, contributing not only to my personal healing but also laying the foundation for my certification journey later on.

As the sessions continued, I developed a close bond with Gail, sharing with her my lack of comprehension and resonance about religion. My analytical mind wanted to know who wrote the Bible, how many times had it been rewritten and interpreted, why is this or that considered a sin, why are there so many different types of religions, what really happens after death, why do I think we've lived other lives— I mean, the list goes on.

Gail recommended a book, "Journey of Souls," by Michael Newton, Ph.D. Here is a brief synopsis of the book:

> *"Journey of Souls" is a groundbreaking book by Dr. Michael Newton that explores the realm of life between lives through the lens of spiritual regression. Drawing on years of*

hypnotherapy sessions with his clients, Dr. Newton takes readers on a captivating exploration of the soul's journey after death. The book delves into the experiences of individuals who have undergone deep hypnosis and recalled their existence between incarnations, unveiling a comprehensive and intricate depiction of the afterlife. Dr. Newton categorizes and analyzes the common elements of these accounts, revealing a fascinating narrative of the soul's progression, spiritual growth, and interactions with guides and fellow souls. "Journey of Souls" challenges conventional notions of the afterlife and offers profound insights into the purpose of our earthly existence, providing a thought-provoking and enlightening perspective on the eternal journey of the soul.

After immersing myself in the pages of that book, a profound sense of clarity came over me, connecting with a calmness that reached into the intricacies of life and the mysteries surrounding death. This book served as a driving force for a newfound understanding, guiding me through a healing process and unraveling answers to a multitude of lingering questions. I had an "Ah-ha" moment, indicating the discovery of the profound truths I had sought regarding religion, the afterlife, and spirituality.

Finally, everything seemed to fall into place, and personally, I consider this book a monumental force in facilitating my healing journey from grief as well as connecting with spirituality. I've suggested or shared my own copies of this book—often repurchasing it—to numerous individuals struggling with loss. Without exception, the feedback has consistently been overwhelmingly positive, with expressions of amazement, gratitude, and appreciation for the recommendation. While it might resonate with some and not with others, I believe it's worth giving it a try.

"Hiking is not just a journey through nature; it's a pilgrimage of the soul where the trail becomes a therapist and the mountains mend our spirit."

-SHAUNA JUDNICH

My love for hiking and the outdoors has been ingrained in me since childhood, growing up in a family that often went camping, fishing, boating, and had outdoor adventures with friends and family. During my decade in the military, I was fortunate to spend four years stationed in Everett, Washington, where the hikes in the Pacific Northwest held a truly magical allure.

By the time I reached this stage of my healing journey, having spent 16 years in the desert, my passion for hiking had taken a backseat. Although I had explored a few trails in the desert, I wasn't as dedicated to hiking as I once had been. Despite this, I still had my favorite desert trails and many yet to be explored.

I also hadn't completely revived my love for the gym and being a 'gym junkie,' but I recognized the importance of staying physically active and that movement was needed. Being outdoors became my remedy—a refreshing and grounding experience that helped me stay present amid life's challenges.

One particular local hike we have is called 'The Cross Trail.' It ranges from 2.2 miles (with a quick steep incline) to about 3.5 miles (easier incline) depending on which route you take. At the top is a 30 ft cross that illuminates at night and has a metal box attached to it with a notebook and pen for anyone to share their thoughts.

This trail became an annual pilgrimage for me on each anniversary of my dad's death. I started painting rocks to leave at the cross, always writing little affirmations of love in the notebook, which I fondly imagined I was sending up to my dad through the cross.

The first time I did the hike on the anniversary, I actually did it solo. At the time, my fitness level was subpar for hiking. Hell, let's not sugarcoat it, it was subpar for anything; I was totally out of shape. However, my determination outweighed my physical condition, and I was determined to complete the hike.

I painted this cute scene on a rock of a light blue sky, a couple of puffy white clouds, and one single red heart balloon, floating in the air as if it were sending love up above. It wasn't a masterpiece by any means, and truthfully, the point of the rock wasn't about artistic perfection; rather, it served as an expression of my emotions at the time.

Opting for the shorter route to the cross, I faced a swift and steep incline for the initial half of the trail. Mentally, I divided it into three sections of steep climbs, anticipating breaks at each point before the trail gradually leveled out.

Despite making it through the first two inclines, barely breathing, I hit a wall at the third incline. Out of breath and frustrated, I said, 'Fuck this, I'm going back down.' Disappointment, as well as tears, welled up as I contemplated my defeat.

However, my perspective shifted as I glanced ahead on the trail, about 100 feet away—an elderly woman was hiking up with a walker! I couldn't believe it! My next thought was, 'Oh, hell no!' And my determination kicked in; I swiftly passed the woman with the walker, offering a quick 'excuse me,' and eventually reached the cross. Despite being completely out of breath and delirious, I made it, pausing only briefly to drop off my rock for my dad. Then I ran all the way back down.

Funny what motivates, or better yet, inspires you, huh?

Given that the 'Cross Trail' hike is a local favorite, I resumed hiking it more frequently to regain my hiking stamina. About two weeks later, I hiked it again and noticed that my rock was missing from the area where I had left it, amongst other painted rocks that had been left there.

For a brief moment, a tinge of sadness and surprise swept over me, considering someone might have taken my rock. Despite my search, I realized that maybe someone else needed it more. The rock had already served its purpose for me when I left it there two weeks ago. Perhaps someone else stumbled upon it, resonated with it, or needed its message for their own reasons. I hoped it brought them some comfort.

And that's when I knew I was beginning to heal.

Over time, I began painting rocks not only for myself but also for others who had experienced the loss of loved ones, as well as for other friends and family who passed away. The process itself became therapeutic; as I painted them at home, I felt an outpouring of love or compassion, depending on whether they were for my loved ones or for friends who had lost someone. By then, I also believed that this energy could be transmitted to the beyond.

Before I knew it, I had formed a hiking tribe—consisting of my husband, kids, friends, and family—who joined me at various times. I found the trails became a sacred space, almost like a moving meditation, where my mind would finally unwind and I could temporarily leave behind the shadows of the recent past. I started to see each incline as representing a struggle—a metaphorical ascent of my trauma and troubles, and every descent, a surrender—and acknowledgment that healing often involves letting go. I'll be totally honest here, some of the struggle was just physically getting up the damn mountain, and I proclaimed each time I was going to quit smoking.

Hiking, beyond being a physical activity, has the remarkable ability to serve as a therapeutic journey for healing. Whether navigating personal challenges, seeking solace, or simply striving for well-being, the trails offer a unique space for rejuvenation and self-discovery.

If you're embarking on a healing journey, here are some factors to think about, particularly concerning hiking, as you explore different avenues to support your personal healing process:

- **Nature's Healing Embrace:** The natural world becomes an expansive canvas for healing. Surrounded by towering trees, open skies, and the earth beneath, depending on the area you go to, hikers find themselves embraced by the soothing arms of nature. The sensory experience of the outdoors becomes a soothing balm for the soul.

- **Rhythmic Release of Stress:** The rhythmic cadence of hiking serves as a meditative rhythm. Each step becomes a deliberate release of stress, a gradual shedding of the burdens carried. The trail's gentle undulations mirror the ebb and flow of life's challenges.

- **Mindful Presence on the Trail:** Hiking invites a mindful presence. As footsteps navigate uneven terrain, the mind engages with the immediate surroundings, temporarily letting go of the noise and distractions of daily life. This mindfulness fosters a connection between the physical and mental realms.

- **Reflection in Every Stride:** The act of hiking encourages reflection. The changing scenery, from lush valleys to panoramic vistas, provides a backdrop for introspection. With every stride, individuals may find themselves contemplating life, seeking clarity, and discovering a renewed sense of purpose.

- **Physical Wellness and Balance:** Beyond the mental and emotional aspects, hiking contributes to physical well-being. The cardiovascular exercise, muscle engagement, and exposure to fresh air promote a holistic sense of balance. The body, mind, and spirit synchronize in the rhythmic dance of the trail.

- **Connection with Others and Community:** While hiking can be a solitary endeavor, the presence of supportive companions can enhance the healing process. Shared stories, shared silences, and the collective experience of nature create a communal bond that aids in the shared healing journey.

- **Adaptability to Personal Needs:** One of the beauties of hiking for healing is its adaptability. Trails cater to various fitness levels and preferences, allowing individuals to choose a path that aligns with their needs. From gentle strolls to challenging ascents, each trail offers its own therapeutic benefits. If you feel like you're out of shape or can't go very far, start with a walk or an easy trail that fits your fitness level. You'd be surprised how quickly you can move up, once you start.

- **Exploration of Inner Strength:** Hiking becomes a metaphor for the exploration of inner strength. Conquering inclines, navigating obstacles, and persevering through the journey symbolize the resilience required in facing life's challenges. The summit, a metaphorical achievement, represents personal victories.

- **Embracing the Present Moment:** This is my personal favorite part - the trail's ever-changing scenery prompts a heightened awareness of the present moment. Each step is an invitation to be fully present, letting go of worries about the past or future. In this state of mindful awareness, individuals often find a sense of peace.

- **A Journey, not a Destination:** Hiking for healing underscores the importance of the journey itself.

While reaching a summit or completing a trail is fulfilling, the true essence lies in the process. The continuous movement forward, the exploration, and the evolution on the path contribute to a sense of personal growth.

Whether it was meandering through wooded paths, summiting peaks, or traversing coastal trails, the act of hiking became a transformative journey for my healing. It allowed me an opportunity to connect with myself, find solace in nature's peaceful beauty, and embrace the therapeutic rhythm of the trail. The healing journey, much like the trails themselves, is an ever-unfolding adventure.

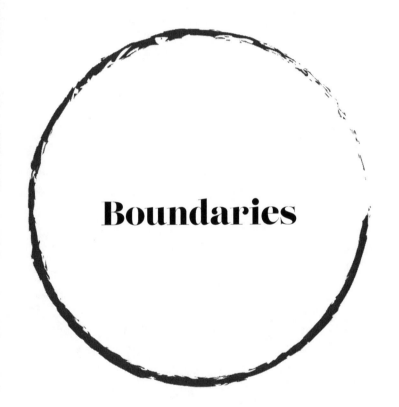

Boundaries

In the past, establishing boundaries was rare for me. However, throughout this journey, I began incorporating them, realizing that certain individuals in my life, intentionally or not, triggered distress, brought negative energy, and couldn't fully comprehend the path of my grief and healing. Some seemed oblivious to the hurtful impact of their words or actions, while others needed to introspect and acknowledge the possibility of embarking on their own healing journey.

As you emerge from the storm, you may find that you have less in common with individuals who have been part of your life for an extended period. Sometimes, to truly evolve and create space for healing and growth, it becomes necessary to release what hinders your progress, and that may involve distancing yourself from certain people.

> "If you don't address healing from your trauma, you may unintentionally burden others who are not responsible for it."
>
> —SHAUNA JUDNICH

As disheartening as it may be, there comes a point where self-preservation may seem like selfishness, but it's necessary. In my experience, if someone didn't contribute to my growth and instead led me backward, away from the path serving my greater good, I had to limit their access. My focus was on progressing and healing, not only from my grief and life's traumas but also from the person I used to be.

It's important to note that this doesn't characterize them as bad or negative people. They were simply on a different path than I was. I still hold immense love for them, and I genuinely hope they find all the love, health, and happiness in life. However, at this point, they weren't contributing to my personal growth or aiding in my healing.

Establishing boundaries during grief is essential for safeguarding your well-being and navigating the grieving process at your own pace. Here are some recommendations on how to set and communicate boundaries during this challenging time:

- **Communicate Openly:** Clearly communicate your needs, limitations, and boundaries to friends, family, and colleagues. Let them know what you can and cannot handle at any given moment.

- **Identify Your Limits:** Reflect on your emotional and physical limits. Understand what situations or interactions may be too overwhelming or draining for you, and be prepared to set boundaries accordingly.

- **Say No When Needed:** It's okay to say no to invitations, requests, or obligations that you feel are beyond your capacity at the moment. Give yourself the space to prioritize your well-being.

- **Take Time for Yourself:** Carve out alone time for self-reflection, rest, and self-care. Grieving is a personal journey, and you may need time alone to process your emotions.

- **Establish Social Media Boundaries:** Consider setting boundaries around social media. You may choose to limit your exposure to certain types of content or take a break from social media altogether if it becomes overwhelming.

- **Educate Others About Your Needs:** Help others understand your grieving process and the support you need. If you need time alone, let them know. If you prefer to talk about your loved one, communicate that as well.

- **Set Work Boundaries:** If you're working, communicate with your employer about your situation. Discuss any adjustments or accommodations that might help you manage your workload during this challenging time.

- **Seek Professional Support:** Consider working with a grief counselor or therapist who can help you navigate your emotions and provide guidance on setting healthy boundaries.

- **Create Physical Boundaries:** Designate personal spaces where you can retreat and have some solitude when needed. Communicate to others that you may need moments of privacy.

- **Be Kind to Yourself:** Recognize that your needs may change from day to day. Be flexible and compassionate with yourself as you navigate through the ups and downs of grief.

- **Removing Toxic Relationships:** Acknowledging when certain individuals may be causing more distress than support and making the difficult decision to distance yourself from toxic relationships. This could involve limiting contact or, in more severe cases, cutting ties to create a healthier environment for your healing.

Remember that setting boundaries is an ongoing process, and it's okay to adjust them as needed. People who care about you will likely appreciate your honesty and respect your boundaries. Taking care of yourself during grief is essential, and establishing clear boundaries is a crucial aspect of self-care.

Breathwork

> "With each intentional breath, healing becomes an intimate conversation with the self. Inhale self-compassion, exhale surrender."
>
> —SHAUNA JUDNICH

I'm always open to exploring new modalities for healing. Despite making significant progress at this point, I believed in the 'more the merrier' philosophy and decided to give breathwork a try. It had always intrigued me, and I had practiced shorter methods on my own for years, but had never tried an actual guided session in person.

Breathwork can offer several benefits for individuals coping with trauma or grief, which is why I wanted to try a more advanced form of the modality. While it's important to note that breathwork is not a substitute for professional mental health care, it can be a complementary practice that supports overall well-being. Here are some potential benefits of breathwork for trauma or grief:

- **Regulation of the Nervous System:** Trauma and grief can dysregulate the autonomic nervous system, leading to heightened states of arousal or persistent feelings of numbness. Breathwork, especially techniques focused on deep and intentional breathing, can help regulate the autonomic nervous system, promoting a sense of balance between the sympathetic and parasympathetic branches.

- **Grounding and Presence:** Many breathwork practices emphasize mindfulness and present-moment awareness. This can help individuals connect with the present and ground themselves, reducing the intensity of traumatic memories or overwhelming grief.

- **Emotional Release:** Breathwork may facilitate the release of stored emotions. By focusing on the breath, individuals can create a safe space for the expression and processing of emotions related to trauma or grief. This release can be cathartic and contribute to emotional healing.

- **Increased Self-Awareness:** Breathwork often involves paying close attention to the breath and bodily sensations. This heightened awareness can provide insights into the connection between emotions and physical experiences, fostering a greater understanding of one's own internal processes.

- **Stress Reduction:** Trauma and grief can lead to heightened stress levels. Breathwork techniques, such as diaphragmatic breathing or rhythmic breathing, can activate the relaxation response, reducing overall stress and promoting a sense of calm.

- **Improved Sleep:** Many people dealing with trauma or grief experience difficulties with sleep. Breathwork can help induce a state of relaxation, making it easier for individuals to fall asleep and experience more restful sleep.

- **Empowerment and Control:** Engaging in breathwork empowers individuals by giving them a sense of control over their physiological and emotional responses. This empowerment can be particularly beneficial for those who feel a loss of control due to traumatic experiences.

- **Enhanced Resilience:** Regular breathwork practice may contribute to increased resilience over time. It can help individuals develop coping mechanisms and a greater capacity to navigate challenging emotions.

After coming across an advertisement on Facebook or Instagram for a breathwork facilitator hosting a large session in the banquet room of a local hotel, I took advantage of the opportunity, considering it was both affordable and convenient.

Honestly, I had no clear expectations of what would come of it. While I had engaged in easy, brief methods on my own and followed short guided sessions through apps and YouTube, what I experienced during this session was unlike anything before. Despite a brief overview of what it entailed, I signed up without a full understanding of what to expect or what the experience would be like.

I had invited a friend who had never attended one either, and as we entered the banquet room, I felt a bit overwhelmed. There were at least 125-150 people there, all finding space on the floor—some with roll-up mats, others with blankets and pillows, even wearing pajamas, creating an atmosphere reminiscent of a high school "lock-in." You might have to look that up too. Again, the 80s...

Anyways, my friend and I brought a small pillow, yoga mat, and eye mask as the ad had suggested. We secured a spot up front and began getting settled. The room was quite noisy, as you can imagine, with that many people packed in. Almost every square inch of the place was occupied.

As the facilitator approached the front of the room, he instructed us to lie down on our backs, put on our eye masks, and get comfortable for what he promised would be a wild ride. He briefly explained the different stages of the session, touched on what might surface individually—such as emotions or memories—and reminded us to embrace and release whatever came up, as that was the purpose of being there.

So there we were, in a sea of people, lying on the floor with eye masks on, and the session began with loud music, a blend of tribal and electronic with a driving beat. He started speaking, guiding us to prepare for the breathing pattern discussed earlier. The music intensified, and he instructed us to breathe more intensely, in a specific rhythmic pattern.

He began discussing the need to release traumas, emotions, and accumulated emotional baggage from our bodies. He demonstrated the recommended breathing sounds, synchronized with the flowing music. The breathing pattern was intense, and he had offered tips at the outset for handling possible side effects from such a breathing pattern.

Engaged in maintaining pace and absorbing his guidance for an emotional release, I wasn't prepared for the unexpected turn of events. From the back corner, there was a cry—a blend of a sob and a scream, a reverberating wail—that quite literally filled the room. My eyes instinctively opened under my eye mask, and internally, I thought, "What. The. Fuck. Was. That?"

The facilitator came through the speaker, urging, "Yes, yes, just let it go," and people did just that. Not only from the back corner but throughout the entire room! Surrounded by sobs, cries, and even screams, I found myself immersed in a flood of emotions. The combined feelings created an inescapable atmosphere, kind of enveloping everyone into this emotional bubble. This emotional outpouring persisted for another 20 minutes.

And that's when I began to cry.

The tears didn't manifest outwardly; instead, they trickled down my face with a few quivers, and soon, I found myself flat-out bawling. And it wasn't because my breathing had bypassed my conscious mind and was delving into the deep layers of my own emotions and traumas. Instead, as I lay there in the middle of this experience, surrounded by cries, I began to wonder.... What happened to that person, or that one, or to all of them that I heard. What has happened in their life that they are having such a profound and outward release?

That's how resounding it was. So yeah, for the last 20 minutes of the session, I laid there, cried, and pondered the stories of the others. I never experienced a personal release, nor did I continue the prescribed breathing pattern. The perks, or perhaps the detriment, of being an empath.

Once it concluded, my friend and I gathered our belongings. I attempted to tidy up my tear-streaked face from the emotional experience, and we took a couple of pictures with the facilitator before leaving. My initial reaction, which I shared with my friend, was that the session would have been better, at least for me, if it had been like a "Silent Disco." When she asked what that meant, I explained: everyone wears headphones, hearing the same thing, allowing for a more personal experience without being influenced by everyone else's emotions. That setup would have been more suitable for someone like me or others with sensory issues.

Needless to say, I left without the intended experience, and surprisingly, I was okay with that.

My friend, who I brought with me, decided to pursue a career as a breathwork facilitator. Although I had contemplated a similar path, I was still engrossed in various other trainings. Therefore, I offered my assistance in supporting her journey.

After she became certified, I contributed to brainstorming, writing projects, advertising efforts, creative concepts for client gifts, and eventually, with setup and class assistance. During each session I assisted in, I shared my story from my initial experience, emphasizing that readiness was crucial for a complete experience. I encouraged participants not to worry if they heard an outward cry, assuring them we were there to support and urging them to refocus on their own breathing and experience. Many found this insight invaluable, appreciating the awareness beforehand.

Her training encompassed a different style of breathwork, characterized by a less intense atmosphere, distinct music, script, and breathing pattern. This approach offered a unique experience compared to the first session we attended together.

Later, my friend embraced my idea of incorporating silent headphones. I researched and ordered them, but by the time they arrived, my other commitments prevented my further involvement. Nonetheless, the headphones became a success, transforming the sessions into immersive experiences. My friend has achieved success with her sessions, as have her clients, which is evident in their positive results.

Should you want to explore breathwork group sessions on your healing journey, consider the following tips:

- **Research Different Types of Breathwork:** There are various styles of breathwork, such as Holotropic Breathwork, Wim Hof Method, and Transformational Breath. Research each type to understand their goals and methods.

- **Identify Your Goals:** Determine why you want to engage in breathwork. Whether it's stress relief, emotional release, spiritual exploration, or physical well-being, knowing your goals will help you find a session that aligns with your needs.

- **Seek Qualified Instructors:** Look for sessions led by certified and experienced breathwork instructors. Check their credentials, training, and reviews from other participants.

- **Ask for Recommendations:** Reach out to friends, family, or online communities for recommendations. Personal experiences can provide valuable insights into the effectiveness and style of different breathwork sessions.

- **Consider Group Size:** Some people prefer smaller, intimate groups for a more personalized experience, while others thrive in larger groups. Consider your comfort level and preferences regarding the size of the session.

- **Location and Atmosphere:** Choose a session held in a location that resonates with you. Whether it's a studio, nature setting, or wellness center, the atmosphere can significantly impact your experience.

- **Check for Safety Measures:** Ensure that safety measures are in place, especially if the breathwork involves intense or altered states of consciousness. A qualified facilitator should be capable of managing any challenges that may arise.

- **Trial Sessions:** Attend trial sessions or workshops before committing to a longer program. This allows you to get a feel for the instructor's style and the specific breathwork techniques used.

- **Trust Your Intuition:** Pay attention to your intuition when choosing a breathwork session. If a particular instructor or style resonates with you, it's more likely to meet your needs.

- **Ask Questions:** Don't hesitate to ask the instructor questions about their approach, the structure of the session, and any potential side effects. A transparent and communicative instructor is essential for a positive experience.

Keep in mind that individual preferences vary, making the search for the right breathwork session a personal journey. Trust your instincts and opt for an approach that aligns with your goals and comfort level.

The cost of many group and private sessions has significantly increased. If you are price-conscious, consider looking for Groupon's or ads offering discounts for trial sessions. Additionally, numerous resources are available on YouTube and various apps; consistency is key when incorporating these practices into your routine and understanding your motivations.

For those who prefer a more accessible approach, I've included a few simple, short methods that you can try at home or anywhere. I personally found them useful during stressful work days. These techniques serve as a gentle introduction to breathwork, allowing you to assess if it could be beneficial for you.

TRIANGLE BREATHING

Triangle breathing, also known as "Triangular Breathing" or "Equal Breathing," is a rhythmic breathing exercise that helps promote relaxation and balance. Here's a simple guide to practicing triangle breathing:

- **Inhale (Count of 3):** Start by taking a slow and deep breath in through your nose, counting to three. Focus on filling your lungs completely with air.

- **Hold (Count of 3):** After inhaling, hold your breath for a count of three. Embrace the stillness and pause in your breath.

- **Exhale (Count of 3):** Slowly exhale through your mouth or nose for a count of three. Release the air gradually, allowing any tension to leave your body.

Repeat this cycle for several breaths, maintaining a steady and equal duration for each phase of the breath—inhale, hold, and exhale.

Triangle breathing is a simple yet effective technique that can be practiced anytime, anywhere. It brings attention to the breath, fostering a sense of calm and balance. This exercise is particularly useful for reducing stress, anxiety, and promoting mindfulness.

BOX BREATHING

Box breathing, also known as square breathing, engages the parasympathetic nervous system, promoting a sense of calm and centeredness. It's a portable technique that can be practiced anywhere, providing a quick reset for your mind and body. Here's a simple guide to this calming practice:

- **Inhale (Count of 4):** Begin by taking a slow, deep breath in through your nose, counting to four. Feel your lungs expand and fill with air as you breathe in.

- **Hold (Count of 4):** Once you've inhaled completely, hold your breath for a count of four. Focus on the stillness and the presence of the breath within your body.

- **Exhale (Count of 4):** Slowly exhale through your mouth for a count of four. Feel the release of tension as you expel the air from your lungs.

- **Pause (Count of 4):** After exhaling, hold your breath for another count of four before beginning the next cycle. Embrace the brief pause before the next inhale.

Repeat this sequence for several cycles, gradually allowing your breath to find a natural, calming rhythm.

4-7-8 METHOD

The 4-7-8 breathing method, also known as the "Relaxing Breath," is designed to activate the body's relaxation response, calming the nervous system and promoting a sense of tranquility. Here's a step-by-step guide:

- **Inhale (Count of 4):** Begin by taking a deep breath in through your nose, counting to four silently. Fill your lungs with air, allowing your abdomen to expand as you breathe.

- **Hold (Count of 7):** Hold your breath for a count of seven. Feel the tension dissipate as you embrace the stillness of this pause.

- **Exhale (Count of 8):** Slowly exhale through your mouth for a count of eight. Focus on completely emptying your lungs and releasing any remaining tension.

Repeat this cycle for three to four breaths when starting, gradually increasing the number of cycles as you become more comfortable with the technique.

5-3-3 METHOD

The 5-3-3 breathing method, also known as "Calm Breathing," is a breathing exercise aimed at promoting relaxation and reducing stress, enhancing focus and promoting a sense of tranquility. Here's a simple guide to practicing the 5-3-3 breathing technique:

- **Inhale (Count of 5):** Start by taking a slow, deep breath in through your nose, counting to five. Focus on filling your lungs with air and allowing your abdomen to expand.

- **Hold (Count of 3):** After inhaling, hold your breath for a count of three. Embrace the stillness and maintain a gentle pause in your breath.

- **Exhale (Count of 3):** Slowly exhale through your mouth or nose for a count of three. Release the air gradually, letting go of any tension.

Repeat this cycle for several breaths, maintaining the sequence of inhale, hold, and exhale with a consistent and calm rhythm.

ALTERNATE NOSTRIL BREATHING

Alternate Nostril Breathing, also known as Nadi Shodhana or Anulom Vilom, is a yogic breathing technique that aims to balance the two hemispheres of the brain and promote a sense of calm and focus. Here's a step-by-step guide on how to practice alternate nostril breathing:

- **Comfortable Seated Position:** Sit comfortably with an upright spine. You can sit on a chair or cushion. Relax your shoulders and place your hands on your knees or in a comfortable mudra, such as the Gyan Mudra (thumb and index finger touching).

- **Close Your Eyes:** Close your eyes to enhance your inward focus and concentration.

- **Prepare Your Breath:** Close your right nostril with your right thumb and inhale deeply and slowly through your left nostril. Fill your lungs with air.

- **Switch Nostrils:** Close your left nostril with your right ring finger, release your right nostril, and exhale completely and slowly through your right nostril.

- **Inhale Through the Right Nostril:** Keeping your left nostril closed, inhale deeply and slowly through your right nostril.

- **Switch Again:** Close your right nostril with your right thumb, release your left nostril, and exhale completely and slowly through your left nostril.

- **Repeat the Cycle:** Continue this cycle, inhaling through the opposite nostril after each exhale. This completes one round.

- **Focus on the Breath:** Throughout the practice, focus on the breath and the sensation of air moving through each nostril. The inhalation and exhalation should be smooth and controlled.

- **Equal Duration:** Aim for an equal duration of inhalation and exhalation for each nostril. You can gradually increase the duration as you become more comfortable with the practice.

- **Complete the Practice:** Finish the practice by ending with an exhale through your left nostril. Then, open both nostrils and sit quietly for a moment, observing the effects.

Alternate Nostril Breathing is renowned for its calming and balancing effects on the nervous system. It's often used as a preparatory practice for meditation or as a tool to alleviate stress and anxiety. Regular practice can bring about a sense of mental clarity and overall well-being.

Mindset

> "Grief is a journey through the valleys of the soul, and in the process of shifting our mindset, we climb the mountains of resilience. Each step echoes with the mantra that healing is not the absence of pain but the triumph over it."
>
> -SHAUNA JUDNICH

The experience of grief is like a dance between your thoughts and emotions. Your mind tries to make sense of the loss by thinking about memories and reflecting on the past, hoping to find closure. Meanwhile, your heart feels the emotional side of grief, experiencing sadness, longing, and pain. Your heart might ache for the person you lost, and you could battle with emptiness and loneliness.

It's a complex journey of the mind and heart working together. These interconnected aspects shape each other as individuals continue through the grieving process, resulting in a diverse range of thoughts and emotions that are integral to the path of healing and acceptance.

Some might underestimate the role of mindset in overcoming grief or trauma, but in my experience, it plays a pivotal role. The key lies in maintaining a balance between the mind and heart, with your mindset residing in the middle.

In the challenging years following my dad's death, and before acquiring the tools and knowledge on my healing journey, my mindset leaned towards suppression. I aimed to be strong, not just for myself but for everyone around me. I was always perceived as the strong and independent one, the person who could handle shit myself. However, I was never truly "seen," neither by others nor by myself.

The trial years kept me locked in a narrow mindset focused on seeking justice, suppressing almost everything else. That's why I often cried alone at night. I held a fixed mindset about who I should be. I don't place blame on myself or others who adopt such thinking during traumatic times. Grief and trauma are challenging, clouding our judgment and making it difficult to discern the impact of our mindset on our well-being.

Looking back, I wish I had the awareness to openly and freely embrace my emotions during those times. I believe it could have assisted me in navigating challenging experiences and alleviated the weight of an already heavy burden. Because of that, I've included some potential mindset shifts that may prove beneficial during periods of grief or trauma:

- **Acceptance of Emotions:** Shift from suppressing or avoiding emotions to accepting and allowing yourself to feel. Understand that grief and trauma bring a range of emotions, and it's okay to experience them.

- **Self-Compassion:** Move from self-blame or harsh self-judgment to self-compassion. Understand that grieving or coping with trauma is a process, and it's important to treat yourself with kindness and understanding.

- **Embracing Support:** Shift from isolation to seeking and accepting support. Understand that reaching out to friends, family, or professional help can provide valuable assistance during challenging times.

- **Growth Mindset:** Move from a fixed mindset to a growth mindset. See challenges as opportunities for personal growth and resilience, acknowledging that you can learn and adapt through difficult experiences.

- **Living in the Present:** Shift from dwelling on the past or worrying about the future to focusing on the present moment. Mindfulness and staying in the present can help manage overwhelming thoughts and emotions.

- **Reframing Perspectives:** Try to shift from negative thinking patterns to reframing perspectives. Look for positive aspects or opportunities for growth even in the midst of grief or trauma.

- **Understanding Change:** Move from resisting change to understanding that change is a part of life. Recognize that adapting to new circumstances is a natural process and can lead to personal transformation.

- **Creating Meaning:** Shift from a sense of meaninglessness to actively creating meaning. Find purpose or meaning in your experiences, whether through personal growth, helping others, or pursuing new passions.

- **Embracing Impermanence:** Move from a sense of permanence to embracing impermanence. Understand that emotions, situations, and life itself are constantly changing, allowing room for healing and recovery.

- **Focusing on Control:** Shift from dwelling on what you can't control to focusing on what you can control. This can help regain a sense of agency and empowerment during challenging times.

It's important to note that everyone copes differently, and these mindset shifts may not be one-size-fits-all. Seeking professional support, such as therapy or counseling, can provide additional guidance and assistance in navigating grief or trauma.

Loss After Healing

"Does death scare me? It does, but not my death specifically. It's the thought of losing those I love and their absence in my life that I fear the most."

-SHAUNA JUDNICH

STEPHANIE

In 2017, I was trying out the whole "Snapchat" thing and sent a picture to my friend, Stephanie. Here's how that went:

Me: sent a picture of myself through Snapchat.

Stephanie: (through Snapchat): 'Are you wearing a toga?'

Me, thinking, WTF, who asks that?!: 'Ummm… no.'

Stephanie: 'It looks like you're wearing a toga.'

Me: 'I'm lying on a pillow… my toga is at the dry cleaners at the moment.'

Stephanie: 'Touché, bitch!'

I'm crying laughing writing this now because it just depicts us, as friends, to a tee. A couple of smart asses with a banter like no other. The amazing part of this section is how we came to be friends in the first place as well as the years of friendship that followed.

From 2008 to 2010, I served as a community service officer for a local police department. My responsibilities included processing crime scenes, taking reports for various incidents like theft, burglary, runaways, missing persons, and handling traffic collision reports, which was my least favor-ite, amongst other duties.

One night in August 2008, I responded to a traffic collision involving two cars. One car had a couple of teenage boys, and in the other, there were individuals who were intoxi-cated. I assisted the teenage boys, one of whom had glass in his mouth. While waiting for the ambulance, I learned that one of the boys, named Matt, attended the same high school as my son. Feeling a connection, I helped him remove the glass and stayed with them until they were taken to the hospital, providing support and keeping them at ease during an understandably stressful situation.

The following day, I reached out to Matt's mom to check on his well-being. I mentioned that my son also attended the same school, and I felt compelled to follow up. She graciously expressed her gratitude, and after a brief chat, we ended the conversation. That was the extent of that interaction.

Fast forward to 2011, 3 years later. A new family moved in across the street from us in our community. They had 4 boys and one of them (Nick) was in the same freshman class as my daughter, so she knew him and would go and hang out at his house from time to time. I finally decided one day that maybe I should go over and meet the mom - because yes, I am THAT mom, but that's another story.

I went over and introduced myself and we stood outside chatting for a few and then she asked, 'What's your last name,' because I had only given my first. I said, 'Judnich.' She lit up and said, 'You've got to be fucking kidding me... Officer Judnich?' I was a little surprised because I had been out of the Police Department for a year by then, but I said, 'Yeah, I was.' She ran in the house and came back out with that police report card with my name written on it and said, 'You're my new best friend.'

And that's how we became best friends.

Through the years, we spent so much time together, having coffee, bitch sessions, supporting each other during trying times, did I mention coffee, so much coffee, cheering for each other during triumphant moments, laughing, crying and all the things that go into the making of a beautiful and authentic friendship. I have so many great stories that are funny, loving and depict the true essence of our friendship, but it would take me writing another book to tell you all about what a truly amazing friend and person Stephanie was. She was also a great supporter after my dad was killed and during the trial years, I will never forget that.

At some point in our friendship, Stephanie and her family moved two hours away, and later, they relocated 3.5 hours away to another state. Despite the distance, we remained in constant contact—seeing each other occasionally, talking on the phone, texting, Instagram and I have so many Facebook posts to and from that show up in memories that I'm ever so grateful for. Needless to say, Snapchat never really clicked with us.

On Aug 27, 2022, as I sat in front of my favorite coffee shop, waiting for my mobile order to be done, I got a phone call from Stephanie's son, Nick. I thought it was odd that he was calling me and hoped that he was ok.

He wasn't - and then - neither was I.

He informed me his mom had passed away. I thought by then I had a decent grip on death, life after death and grief. I was wrong. Although I didn't fall down the hole, I found myself immersed in it, gripping the top, clinging to hope, just trying to hold on and not fall to the bottom, determined not to be consumed by grief's depths.

I spent a few days in bed, I cried, I contacted mutual friends who maybe had not heard and I reflected on the beautiful friendship I had with her. I also picked up my copy of Journey of Souls and started re-reading it. Interestingly, I had recommended this book to Stephanie the year before when her husband passed away. She often sent me texts thanking me for the recommendation and expressing how much it helped her.

Re-reading parts of that book brought me solace that Stephanie was undoubtedly in my soul group and I found comfort knowing that I'd reunite with her at some point again. I recommended the book to her boys and hoped that it would offer them some comfort as it had for their mother. I also went back to the basics of mindfulness, breathwork, being present in the moment and feeling my feelings when they arose.

The point here is not that you "get over or get through" death, pain or trauma more easily as time goes on, but that if you do look inward, if you take yourself on a healing journey during a profound loss or trauma, you will eventually be able to process and handle things differently once you've provided yourself with the necessary tools. And sometimes you won't.

Although Stephanie wasn't a family member, and you might be thinking that's why I was able to hold on and not be consumed, she was family to me. I hope that you also have those kinds of friends in your life - the kind that are more family than blood relatives could ever be.

DANNY

On August 7, 2022, my daughter experienced the loss of her younger half-brother, Danny, who was the son of her biological father. This was an incredibly challenging moment for me as a mother, especially because my daughter had just relocated from California to New York on that very day. I had to wait until she landed safely and got to her temporary Airbnb to deliver the heartbreaking news, as I didn't want her to learn about it in any other way.

Despite the split between my ex-husband and I when my daughter was only one year old (she was now 26), we had maintained a pretty decent friendship through the years. I was also acquainted with his wife, Isabel. The previous year, my daughter and Danny had reconnected, fostering a beautiful sibling connection through frequent conversations, music sharing, and book recommendations. This was remarkable considering they hadn't seen each other or communicated much in approximately 14 years.

Danny was going through a tough period, mainly due to a recent breakup, and was struggling with his own grief and pain. My daughter, concerned about his well-being, talked to him regularly and expressed her worries to me about his use of drugs and alcohol as coping mechanisms. As a result, I increased my contact with my ex-husband and his wife, attempting to provide some support during this difficult time.

Unfortunately, on the morning my daughter arrived in New York City, Danny's enlarged heart gave out, and he passed away. At 23, he was a gentle giant and a beautiful soul who lost his way.

Understandably, my daughter was devastated. I was 3,000 miles away, and all I could do was be there for her, just as she had been for me, through our shared distance. It was during this time that I truly began to apply what I had learned to help others.

I not only supported my daughter but also extended help to my ex-husband and his wife. We spoke almost daily, and I sent them a copy of the "Journey of Souls" book. I also inquired if they were open to Emotion Code sessions, hoping it might create some space for healing. They gratefully welcomed any support and assistance.

I want to emphasize that I don't make these suggestions lightly. I'm not suggesting that Emotion Code sessions, books, breathwork, or any tools mentioned in this book, or really anything, can suddenly alleviate the pain and sorrow that a parent experiences upon losing a child—or any loss, for that matter. **Not at all**. However, based on my experience, these modalities and tools can possibly offer some mental clarity, an internal release that lightens the emotional and physical burden. This, in turn, has the potential for creating space for acceptance and healing.

The reason I believe this is because of what I witnessed through Isabel after losing her son.

During the first year after Danny's death, we spoke constantly over the phone, sometimes daily and twice a day even. I will never try to assume what a parent is going through or have gone through with the loss of a child. I find it unimaginable. Because of that, I mainly wanted to be a support system for Isabel as she and her husband (my ex-husband) had very distinctly different ways of going through the grieving process, as many people do. There is no right or wrong way.

I found a deep connection with Isabel due to our similar thought processes, empathetic nature, and emotional responses. Having personally experienced the challenges of feeling unsupported in grief, partly due to my own suppression and partly because people often struggle to provide effective assistance, I recognized the importance of being a supportive presence for her.

Isabel's willingness to entertain the suggestions presented in this book, as well as her participation in Emotion/Body Code sessions, revealed a remarkable openness to healing. Witnessing her resilience in the face of such unimaginable loss left me in awe, as I acknowledged again my inability to fully comprehend the depths of a parent's sorrow when losing a child.

Isabel has instilled in me a renewed sense of optimism for the healing process. While she traversed some of the same paths in her quest for answers as I did, she went above and beyond, frequently sharing insights and discoveries that had not yet crossed my mind.

Undoubtedly, there are days and moments when the harsh reality of her loss still hits her profoundly—how could it not? Nevertheless, observing her navigate through her own storm on this journey has been truly extraordinary.

She has undergone a transformative evolution, emerging as a different person from the one I knew before the tragedy, as is often the case with profound loss and grief. Witnessing her resilience and growth has been remarkable.

Although Isabel expresses gratitude and credits me for her current state, the truth is that I merely offered some tools, empathy, and support. She, on the other hand, undertook the challenging work herself, and I am genuinely thankful to have played a role in witnessing her progress unfold.

FAMILY, FRIENDS AND FUR BABIES

The year 2023 brought a shitstorm of loss. Just two days into the new year, my second cousin, Ken, died in a snowmobile accident. The world, as well as our family, was left in shock. If you know of or knew Ken, you know he's done some of the craziest things. So, this was truly shocking.

My initial thought was his family- his wife and kids. We were distant cousins, having only spent a few holidays together, but as much as the world admired his talents, I admired what I was so fortunate to witness - the love and adoration he clearly had for his wife and kids.

In an effort to offer solace, I sent a card along with a recommendation of the book *"Journey of Souls"* and a printout of the Reddit response I mentioned earlier in the grief section. In the card, I expressed my wish that they continue pursuing what they loved as they navigated through their grief. This sentiment stemmed from my own experience and observing my family struggle to embrace life and seemingly giving up really living it, after my dad's tragic death.

I realize it might sound cliché, the idea of giving up on living life amid grief, but looking back now, I understand that those who have departed wouldn't wish for us to live that way. We can't alter the past, and eventually, we must find a way to move forward. Drawing from my own experience, I felt compelled to recommend to Ken's family that, to weather their own storm, they should continue engaging in the activities they loved while going through their grief journey. I believed it would bring them closer to him, and I knew they had a strong support network that would always be there for them.

The relentless shitstorm persisted in the early hours of Ken's memorial in January 2023, an event I couldn't attend due to illness. Shockingly, Ken's older brother, my cousin Steve, passed away that morning.

Had it not happened, I would find it hard to believe. It was natural for my mind to wander to the familiar question... What. The. Fuck? The year had just begun, and we had already lost two family members—two brothers, no less.

I had a closer relationship with Steve, spending more time with him over the years, especially during my visits to our cousin Lora's house or him stopping by mine on his way to see his kids. Lora shared a close bond with both Ken and Steve, but her connection with Steve was particularly strong, given their proximity. They had been having dinner and game nights on Fridays for years, Steve helped with handyman things around her house and both played pivotal roles in caring for Steve's mom before her passing. He was more like a brother to her than a cousin.

Amidst grief once again, I shifted my focus to Lora, under-standing the depth of her emotions. Despite her strength and realistic outlook on life and death, losing both Ken and Steve so closely together was an immense challenge. I offered a listening ear, comforting sentiments when needed, and tried to be there for her using the tools I had learned.

Grief is challenging when it involves a loved one, but be-ing present for another loved one in intense pain can be heartbreaking. Perhaps it's the empath in me, but reflecting on the past, I don't believe that's the case. My journey had brought me to a point of being fully present, no longer self-ishly focused on myself as I had been in the past, but instead more concerned for Lora and what she was feeling.

Also in January 2023, my husband and I lost our two dogs within weeks of each other, one in a very traumatic way, the other to cancer, and our 21-year-old cat shortly thereafter. Later in the year, my friend Karen succumbed to an aggres-sive cancer, followed by my cousin Cinnamon, who had ini-tially beaten cancer but eventually passed away from another aggressive form. I think we all can agree here—fuck cancer!

I reached out to my daughter after each death in 2023, finding solace in talking to her. She knows me well, accu-rately perceiving when I'm putting on a facade or holding things in. She encouraged me to share anything with her, willingly shouldering the burden. It's interesting how roles shift, and our kids become the ones we turn to for support in such moments.

During my dad's death and the years that followed, she was a tremendous source of support, often coming into my room late at night because she knew I was awake and crying. Despite feeling the loss herself, as it was her grandpa, she remained a pillar of emotional support for me. Even when Stephanie passed away, although physically distant due to being out of state, she continued to offer her emotional support. By the end of 2023, after experiencing all the loss that year, she said she felt like she was becoming "numb to death."

And I wondered -was I too?

Moving
Forward

> "Tragedy and trauma didn't make you stronger. They tore you apart, threw you down a hole, fractured your soul, disrupted your peace and temporarily robbed you of living life. You dug yourself out of that hole by embracing it, acknowledging it, healing from it and moving forward with it."
>
> —SHAUNA JUDNICH

As I reflected on the recurring theme of death in my life, both recent and past, I realized that I hadn't become numb to it. At this point, I had gathered insights and valuable tools for healing. I embraced the understanding that life involves both living and dying. My belief system had expanded to recognize the existence of interconnected soul groups spanning this life, past lives, and those yet to unfold.

I acknowledged that succumbing to the unrelenting grip of grief each time wouldn't change the inevitable loss of loved ones or prevent traumatic events. Pain would persist, but what I refused to surrender while in that abyss was the ability to live and celebrate the lives and love of those I had lost.

And here lies the heart of it: we don't simply move on, but we are compelled to move forward.

I've often encountered the phrase "move on," and I've never been fond of it; in fact, I usually correct people. To me, "move on" carries a sense of detachment. The truth is, you never truly move on.

The term "moving forward," especially in the context of grief, holds a more compassionate and empowering connotation than "moving on." While "moving on" might suggest leaving the past behind or forgetting, "moving forward" implies a gradual and respectful progression through the healing process.

Grief is a complex and individual journey that doesn't necessarily involve abandoning memories or emotions but rather integrating them into one's life. The expression "moving forward" recognizes the significance of the grieving experience and underscores personal growth, resilience, and the ability to navigate life with the lessons learned from the loss.

It conveys the idea that individuals can honor their past while still embracing the potential for a positive and meaningful future. In essence, "moving forward" encourages a forward path that respects the depth and impact of grief, fostering a more supportive and understanding approach to those who are navigating the challenges of loss.

Whether it's trauma, grief from the loss of a loved one, or any other type of pain or damage inflicted upon you, moving on from it might not be feasible. However, moving forward with it is possible. That's the perspective I prefer. You don't have to let it define you, but it did happen, it did affect you, alter you, break you; perhaps it even immobilized you.

Acknowledging it is crucial to moving forward with it, onto the next step, journey, or path. In doing so, there is no limit to your healing and the person you can become.

Forgiveness

I n October of 2020, my sister informed me that the girl who had killed our dad had gotten into some other kind of trouble. She sent me what she found, and with my background, I knew that it was a DUI. I thought, "Wow, 5 years after killing my dad and less than 2 years after being convicted for it, she got a DUI." It was disheartening to realize that, despite the gravity of her actions, she had not learned her lesson.

I went to work once again, calling both the District Attorney's office and probation services. Given that she was still on probation and her initial prison sentence had been set aside when she was sentenced for my dad's death, any violation meant she would be obligated to serve the previously assigned two-year prison term.

Of course, this was during the height of Covid, so navigating the bureaucratic bullshit proved to be quite the task. Government agencies were overwhelmed, and the oversight on her probation violation went unnoticed for a minute. They did, however, realize it when I was done.

Long story short, her probation was deemed violated, and in 2021, she was ordered to serve the initially assigned prison term. Due to the Covid pandemic-related adjustments and California's "good time credit" system, she ended up serving approximately 4-5 months.

There were some who had hoped she would learn a lesson or two in prison. My perspective differed. I wished for this to mark her rock bottom - a period of introspection, a chance for potential transformation, and personal growth.

Upon her release 4-5 months later, I exhaled the breath I had been holding since 2015 and forgave her. Internally, I hoped that she would emerge from prison as an improved individual - one who would embrace accountability, perhaps even advocating against texting and driving, sharing her story to raise awareness.

To be honest, a thought crossed my mind - did she end up with a DUI due to the overwhelming guilt from killing my dad 5 years ago? I considered the possibility that she might have turned to excessive alcohol consumption as a coping mechanism, a reaction some adopt during times of trauma and grief. I didn't find joy in this thought. Again, the empath in me.

I forgave her also because I had come to understand that holding onto resentment only caused me pain; it didn't affect her in any way.

Forgiving those who caused you trauma or pain can have numerous psychological, emotional, and even physical benefits. While forgiveness is a personal choice and not always easy, embracing it can lead to positive outcomes. Here are some potential benefits:

- **Emotional Well-being:** Forgiveness can contribute to improved emotional well-being by reducing feelings of anger, resentment, and bitterness. It allows you to let go of negative emotions that may be holding you back, promoting a sense of inner peace.

- **Reduced Stress:** Holding onto grudges and unresolved emotions can contribute to chronic stress. Forgiveness may help alleviate stress and promote a more relaxed state of mind.

- **Improved Mental Health:** Forgiveness has been associated with lower levels of depression and anxiety. Letting go of negative emotions can positively impact mental health and contribute to overall psychological resilience.

- **Enhanced Relationships:** Forgiving others can improve relationships, whether by rebuilding trust or setting healthy boundaries. It may also lead to more positive interactions and a sense of connection with others.

- **Increased Empathy:** Forgiveness often involves understanding the perspectives of others. This can lead to increased empathy, fostering a more compassionate and understanding approach to people and their actions.

- **Physical Health Benefits:** Research suggests that forgiveness can have positive effects on physical health. Lower levels of stress and improved emotional well-being may contribute to better cardiovascular health and immune function.

- **Personal Growth:** Forgiving others can be a catalyst for personal growth. It encourages self-reflection, resilience, and the development of coping mechanisms, contributing to an overall sense of maturity and wisdom.

- **Freedom from Resentment:** Holding onto resentment can be emotionally exhausting. Forgiveness provides a sense of liberation from the burden of negative emotions, allowing you to move forward with your life.

- **Increased Self-Esteem:** Letting go of resentment and embracing forgiveness can positively impact self-esteem. It reflects strength and self-empowerment, as you choose not to let past experiences define your sense of self-worth.

- **Spiritual and Cultural Benefits:** For some individuals, forgiveness aligns with spiritual or cultural values. It may be seen as a pathway to spiritual growth, reconciliation, or alignment with cultural beliefs about compassion and understanding.

Forgiveness (for other reasons) can be a complex and challenging process, especially during times of grief. Grieving involves a range of emotions, and the need for forgiveness may arise in various ways. Here are some thoughts on forgiveness during grief:

- **Self-Forgiveness:** Grieving individuals often experience guilt or regret about things left unsaid or undone with the deceased person. It's essential to recognize that nobody is perfect, and self-forgiveness is a crucial part of the healing process.

- **Forgiving Others:** Grief can sometimes be intertwined with unresolved issues or conflicts with the person who passed away. Forgiving them, even if they're no longer alive, can help release the emotional burden and allow for healing.

- **Understanding Perspectives:** People may react differently to grief, and some behaviors might be hurtful. Trying to understand the perspective of others, acknowledging their pain, and finding empathy can contribute to the forgiveness process.

- **Communication:** If possible, having open and honest communication with those involved can help in the forgiveness process. Expressing feelings and addressing concerns may lead to understanding and healing.

- **Acceptance:** Forgiveness doesn't necessarily mean condoning or excusing the actions that caused pain. It can be more about accepting the reality of the situation and choosing not to hold onto resentment.

- **Professional Support:** Grief counseling or therapy can be beneficial for navigating complex emotions and facilitating the forgiveness process. A professional can provide guidance and support during this challenging time.

- **Patience with Yourself:** Forgiveness is a gradual process, and it's important to be patient with yourself. Grieving is a unique journey, and everyone moves through it at their own pace.

- **Cultural or Spiritual Guidance:** For some, turning to cultural or spiritual practices can provide a framework for forgiveness. Seeking guidance from religious or cultural leaders can offer support and insights.

It's essential to note that forgiveness is a personal journey, and its benefits may vary for each individual. Additionally, forgiveness does not necessarily mean forgetting or condoning harmful actions; it is about releasing the grip of negative emotions to foster personal growth and well-being. It is a personal journey, and there is no set timeline for when or how it should occur. It's okay to seek support from friends, family, or professionals to navigate the complexities of forgiveness during grief.

Other Tips

SIGNIFICANT EVENTS DURING LOSS

Experiencing grief during significant occasions, such as a wedding, can be incredibly challenging and bittersweet. While the event may be filled with joy, celebration, and love, it can also serve as a poignant reminder of the absence of a loved one who is no longer there to share the moment. The juxtaposition of happiness and sorrow can evoke a range of emotions, from nostalgia and longing to a sense of emptiness and grief. Despite the desire to participate fully in the festivities, there may be moments of sadness or tears as memories of the departed loved one flood in.

I experienced this at my son's wedding. It took place just six weeks after my dad's tragic passing. With plans set, everything paid for, and anticipation built over six months, there was no possibility of postponement.

Despite the sadness, it was a gorgeous desert wedding. So many friends and family collectively showed up to celebrate my son and his now-wife. The weather was ideal for an outdoor wedding, and the reception hall was beautifully decorated. Everything was perfect.

During the reception, an empty chair at our table caught my attention, its significance hitting me like a wave. Tears welled up, cascading down my cheeks, and soon, the entire table of ten family members was in tears. My daughter rushed to embrace me, her tears mingling with mine, followed by my son. Though our table was near the front, close to the bride and groom, I'm unsure if anyone else noticed our emotional moment, but how could they not?

It was a fleeting moment, quickly pulled back together, yet I couldn't shake the feeling of letting sadness momentarily overshadow such a joyous occasion. But suppressing emotions, as I've mentioned, only exacerbates the pain.

Through this experience, I've come to understand the importance of allowing oneself to feel and seek support when needed during such events. Finding solace amidst the celebrations is essential, honoring both the memory of the departed and the joy of the occasion. Reflecting on my journey, I've compiled a list of strategies to navigate grief during special occasions:

- **Acknowledge your feelings:** Allow yourself to feel whatever emotions come up, whether it's sadness, nostalgia, or longing. Suppressing emotions can intensify them later on.

- **Plan ahead:** Anticipate triggers and emotionally charged moments during the event. Prepare coping strategies such as taking breaks, having a support person nearby, or practicing mindfulness techniques.

- **Honor the memory:** Find meaningful ways to honor and remember your loved one during the event. This could include setting up a memorial table, lighting a candle, or sharing stories and memories with others.

- **Set boundaries:** It's okay to decline invitations or limit your participation in certain activities if they feel too overwhelming. Prioritize your well-being and do what feels comfortable for you.

- **Seek support:** Surround yourself with understanding friends and family members who can provide comfort and support during the event. Don't hesitate to lean on them for emotional support or companionship.

- **Practice self-care:** Take care of yourself physically and emotionally leading up to and during the event. Get plenty of rest, eat nourishing foods, engage in activities that bring you comfort and relaxation, and avoid excessive alcohol or substances.

- **Have an exit plan:** Give yourself permission to leave the event if you need a break or if your emotions become too overwhelming. Having an exit strategy in place can help you feel more in control of the situation.

- **Express yourself creatively:** Channel your emotions into creative outlets such as writing, drawing, or crafting. Expressing your feelings in a creative way can be therapeutic and cathartic.

- **Connect with others:** Reach out to others who may be experiencing similar feelings of grief during the event. Sharing your experiences and offering support to one another can create a sense of solidarity and understanding.

- **Seek professional help:** If you find that your grief is overwhelming or interfering with your ability to cope, consider seeking support from a therapist or counselor who specializes in grief and loss. They can provide guidance, validation, and coping strategies to help you navigate this challenging time.

CONVERSATIONS

Navigating conversations with grieving individuals requires sensitivity and empathy. Sometimes it's hard to know exactly what to say in order to express condolences in a supportive and comforting manner, minimizing the risk of inadvertently causing further distress. Grief can be a highly individual and complex experience, and well-intentioned comments may unintentionally miss the mark. From my experiences, the following are some things to avoid saying and potentially better things to say:

Things to Avoid Saying to Someone Who Is Grieving:

- "I know how you feel." **Why to avoid:** Grief is a highly personal experience, and no two people grieve in exactly the same way. Claiming to know their feelings can minimize the uniqueness of their grief.

- "At least they lived a long life." **Why to avoid:** This statement may unintentionally invalidate the person's pain. The length of a loved one's life doesn't necessarily diminish the intensity of grief.

- "They are in a better place now." **Why to avoid:** While well-intentioned, this phrase might be dismissive of the person's grief, as it doesn't acknowledge the immediate pain they are feeling.

- "Everything happens for a reason." **Why to avoid:** This statement can feel dismissive and may not be helpful to someone grappling with the randomness and unfairness of death

- "You need to be strong for others." **Why to avoid:** This places an additional burden on the grieving person, suggesting they should prioritize others over their own emotions.

- "They wouldn't want you to be sad." **Why to avoid:** It implies how the person should or shouldn't feel, which can be invalidating. Grieving is a personal process, and everyone copes differently.

Better Things to Say to Someone Who Is Grieving:

- "I'm so sorry for your loss." **Why it helps:** This simple expression of sympathy acknowledges their pain without assuming you know exactly what they're going through.

- "I'm here for you." **Why it helps:** Offering your presence and support communicates that you are available without imposing expectations on how they should cope.

- "I can't imagine what you're going through, but I'm here to listen." **Why it helps:** Acknowledging the difficulty of their experience while offering a listening ear shows empathy and support.

- "Take all the time you need to grieve; there's no right or wrong way to feel." **Why it helps:** This statement recognizes the individuality of the grieving process and validates their emotions.

- "I remember when [share a positive memory]." **Why it helps:** Sharing a fond memory allows the grieving person to focus on positive aspects and celebrate the life of their loved one.

- "Is there anything specific I can do for you right now?" **Why it helps:** Offering practical help demonstrates your willingness to support them in concrete ways, without making assumptions about their needs.

- "It's okay to feel whatever you're feeling." **Why it helps:** This acknowledges the complexity of grief and reassures the person that their emotions are valid.

- "I'm thinking of you during this difficult time." **Why it helps:** Expressing ongoing concern shows that you are there for them beyond the immediate aftermath of the loss.

Remember, the most important thing is to offer genuine support and empathy. Everyone's grief is unique, so adapt your words based on the individual's preferences and the nature of your relationship with them.

INSIGHT TIMER (APP)

My childhood friend, Eric, suggested to me during a very emotional phone call one night on my journey to try the app - Insight Timer.

It offers many meditations, breathworks, therapeutic music, and more. I found this app extremely helpful during times when my mind wouldn't shut off. I was actually able to meditate using this app, something I hadn't been able to do in the past, which really helped quiet the mind and allowed for a more calming sensation - whether for healing, general stress, or further enlightenment.

They also offer almost 4,000 courses, ranging from guides to deeper sleep, to freeing yourself from blame/resentment, to creating a conscious morning ritual, and so much more. I still use this app to this day and find it very useful for many aspects.

JOURNALING

Once I made it through the anger and began my healing journey, I started writing again. Sometimes, I would simply open a journal and jot down whatever I was feeling because I was still in a mental space where I didn't want to burden anyone. Journaling helped immensely, and I would often cry while writing, which provided a necessary release.

Journaling can be a therapeutic way to process grief. Here are some prompts to help you explore your feelings and thoughts:

- Describe a favorite memory you shared with your loved one.
    - What made that moment special?
    - How does recalling this memory make you feel?
- Write a letter to your loved one.
    - Express your thoughts and emotions as if you were talking directly to them.

- Share anything you wish you had said or wish you could say now.
- Explore the emotions you're feeling.
    - List the emotions you're experiencing, and describe each one in detail.
    - Reflect on how these emotions manifest physically and emotionally.
- Create a timeline of your grief journey.
    - Chart the ups and downs, milestones, and moments of realization since your loss.
    - Reflect on how your feelings have evolved over time.
- Write about the impact of the loss on your daily life.
    - How has your routine changed?
    - Are there specific challenges you've faced in your day-to-day activities?
- Explore the concept of acceptance.
    - What does acceptance mean to you in the context of your grief?
    - How have your feelings about acceptance changed over time?
- Describe a coping mechanism that has been helpful.
    - What activities or strategies have provided some relief?
    - How do these coping mechanisms contribute to your healing process?
- Reflect on the support you've received.
    - Who has been there for you during this time?

- How has their support impacted your grieving process?
- Explore any regrets or unfinished business.
  - Is there something you wish you had said or done differently?
  - How can you find closure or peace regarding any unresolved feelings?
- Write a list of things you're grateful for.
  - Despite the pain, what aspects of your life bring you some comfort or joy?
  - How can focusing on gratitude help you navigate your grief?

Remember, journaling is a personal and introspective process, so feel free to adapt these prompts to suit your needs. There's no right or wrong way to express your feelings, and it's okay to take your time with the process.

#

Hans Christian Andersen once stated, 'Where words fail, music speaks,' and I wholeheartedly agree. Music serves as my love language, and I hold deep admiration for various artists and their ability to evoke profound emotions through lyrics, vocals, and melodies.

When I first wrote 'What a year after death has taught me' as a Facebook post, I accompanied it with a video featuring different pictures of my dad, my family, and moments with him, set to the backdrop of the song 'Chasing Cars' by Snow Patrol.

Just before writing it, I had been driving on a beautiful day in the desert when the song, despite being 11 years old at the time and not frequently heard, started playing. I distinctly recall the instant my dad came to mind.

There's a line in the song that resonated deeply with me. It triggered a recollection of a time when I returned home on leave, and my dad and I worked together to rotate the tires and inspect something under the wheel well of my car. It was just the two of us, lying on the ground, working, talking, and laughing. As the music played, that specific line resonated with a desire to revisit that cherished moment, and I wished we could go back to it.

As soon as I got home, in tears, I wrote out 'What a year after a death has taught me,' created the accompanying video, and shared it on Facebook. The emotional reaction I received from that post was unlike anything I had experienced before.

That song became my 'signs' song. Again, it's an older song, released in 2005 and not played all that often, so every time I hear it, I think, 'I love you too, dad.'

Some people have a hard time with music that reminds them of their loved one. I learned to embrace and cherish it for what it is—a remembrance of love.

SIGNS FROM ABOVE

As I mentioned in the 'Music' section, the song 'Chasing Cars' became a 'sign,' as in a 'sign from above,' for me. As I began to explore and embrace spirituality, continue healing, and connect with those I lost, I started to notice and acknowledge these signs more frequently.

The concept of 'signs from above' is often rooted in spiritual, religious, or metaphysical beliefs. It suggests that external events, symbols, or occurrences are interpreted as meaningful messages or guidance from a higher power, the universe, or divine entities. These signs are thought to manifest in various forms, aiming to communicate insights, reassurance, or direction to individuals.

The interpretation of 'signs from above' can vary widely among different belief systems. Some common manifestations include:

- **Symbolic Objects:** Certain objects or symbols may be perceived as significant, such as feathers, coins, or specific animals. These are often considered messages or reminders of a presence beyond the physical realm.

- **Synchronicities:** Meaningful coincidences or synchronicities in everyday life are often seen as signs. For example, hearing a particular song during a moment of reflection or encountering a repeated number sequence might be interpreted as a message.

- **Dreams:** Dreams are sometimes believed to be a channel through which higher powers communicate. Specific symbols or interactions in dreams may be considered messages or insights.

- **Nature Signs:** Changes in weather, unusual natural events, or encounters with specific elements of nature, like rainbows or particular birds, are sometimes interpreted as signs of guidance or encouragement.

- **Intuitive Insights:** Some people believe that a sense of inner knowing or intuition can be a form of guidance from above. Trusting one's instincts and paying attention to inner feelings may be seen as a way of receiving guidance.

- **Visions or Spiritual Experiences:** Some individuals report having visions or spiritual experiences that they interpret as direct communication from a higher power. These experiences can be highly personal and subjective.

It's important to note that the interpretation of "signs from above" is subjective and can be deeply influenced by cultural, religious, or individual beliefs. Skeptics may view such signs as mere coincidences or products of the human tendency to seek patterns and meaning in random events. Regardless of one's perspective, the belief in signs from above can provide comfort, hope, and a sense of connection for those who find meaning in these manifestations.

Poems

What I Am Not

I am not my trauma, nor the shadow it casts,

I am not the scars that haunt my past.

I am the resilience that courses through my veins,

the strength that rises from life's trials and pains.

I am not the mistakes I've made or the battles I've lost,

I am the wisdom gained and the lessons taught.

I am not defined by who I've been with or the heartaches

that left trails of grief,

I am the love that still resides within my soul, the capacity

to heal and be whole.

I am not chained to the expectations of others, but free to

follow my own path, to discover.

I am not the sum of all my fears and doubts,

but the courage that propels me to seek out the

possibilities,

the dreams, and the light that guides me through the
darkest of nights.

I am not limited by the stories of the past, but
empowered by the future I continue to cast.

I am not confined by the judgment of the world,
but liberated by the authenticity I continue to unfold.

I am the architect of my own destiny,
the navigator of my journey, the force that sets me free.

I am not the labels that society has imposed,
but the unfolding of a spirit that cannot be enclosed.

I am not my trauma, nor the battles I fought,
but the triumph of the human spirit, a resilience widely
sought.

I am not who I was or what I've been through,
but the evolution of a soul reborn and renewed.

I am not the echoes of the past that linger,
but the symphony of hope, faith and strength that grows
stronger.

I am not the sum of my pain, my losses, nor my
mistakes,
but a constellation of love, grace and perseverance that
awakes.

I am not defined by the chapters already written,

but by the courage to embrace the future - unfettered,

unbreakable and unshaken.

I am not my trauma,

but the triumphant survivor,

embracing the journey - fierce, alive and forever thriving.

I will not be defined..... by what I am not.

-Shauna Judnich

Griefs Bodyguard

In the dance of emotions, a complex ballet,

Anger guards grief, keeping tears at bay.

A fierce soldier, a formidable guide,

Yet in its shadow, vulnerability hides.

Release the grip, let emotions flow,

A journey through grief, both high and low.

For in understanding anger's facade,

The heart finds solace, a path that is broad.

So, let anger be acknowledged and understood,

A bodyguard shielding grief as it should.

For in the partnership, a truth unfolds,

That healing begins when the story's told.

-Shauna Judnich

End of the journey

As I reflect on the final page of my journey through grief, I can't help but appreciate the transformative path I traversed since the profound loss that altered the course of my life.

Drawing from the experiences shared within these pages, I encourage fellow travelers to embrace grief as a potent catalyst for personal growth. My hope throughout is that I have offered practical tips from my own experience, as I navigated the turbulent waters of loss, that are helpful, even if in some small way. I want to emphasize the importance of self-compassion, allowing yourself the necessary time and space to grieve at your own pace.

Reflecting on the overarching theme, I want to remind you that grief is not a linear path but a nuanced, evolving process. In these final words, I hope I have conveyed a sense of hope, affirming that even amid the darkest moments, there lies the potential for resilience, strength, and the gradual emergence of a renewed sense of purpose.

As I close this chapter, I recognize that grief will forever be a part of my story, but so too was the capacity for healing and finding meaning in the midst of profound loss.

Acknowledgements

Most people don't like to read this part, but it's actually one of my favorite parts of a book. I love to read about the people in the author's life that inspired, supported and helped them along their journey. Maybe I always liked to read it because I didn't feel like I had those types of people in my life in the past. But here I am… having those people.

My daughter, Sierra - Your constant support and love were an anchor through my grief and challenges. Your presence has illuminated my darkest days, and I am endlessly grateful for you. I often wish I had the wisdom and strength I have now when I faced the challenges of being a young, divorced mom so that I could have been my best self while you were growing up. Our bond has taught me the true essence of unconditional and true love. I hope that by finally fulfilling my goal of writing this book, it will inspire you with your endeavors as much as you've inspired me to complete mine. LYM.

My Husband, Tracy - I extend my heartfelt thanks for the love and support you've consistently shown me in your own unique way. Your willingness to let me navigate my journey without judgment or interference has been invaluable. Allowing me to embrace my true self, with all its complexities, has been pivotal in shaping my current path. I love you, not just for this, but for the multitude of reasons that make you special to me.

My son, Adam and Daughter-in-Law, Melissa - Having a son like you, Adam, brings me immense gratitude. Your genuineness, thoughtfulness, and overall remarkable nature are a source of great pride. Your choice of a life partner, Melissa, who embodies these qualities has enriched my life twofold. I want to express my heartfelt thanks for the love and support throughout the years. I love you both immensely and I am truly blessed to have you in my life.

My mom, Linda - I want to express my gratitude for your enduring love and support, both during this specific time and in the broader journey of life. While I may not have articulated it frequently, I see you as one of the most resilient individuals I know, particularly in navigating the challenges of being widowed twice (my biological dad and the dad that raised me). I truly believe that your strength has been a profound influence on my own resilience. Thank you for being a beacon of strength and love in my life. I love you.

My sister, Amanda and brother, Phillip, my Brother-in-Law, Andy and other family members (uncles, aunts, cousins)- This book is not just a recounting of our tragedy, but a testament to the indomitable spirit that unites our hearts in both sorrow and triumph. I extend my deepest gratitude and love for the warmth and solidarity that have shaped our journey through the shadows. I hope this stands as a tribute to the enduring love that defines our family, a love that triumphs over even the darkest days. I love you all.

Rod S - As a friend of my dad's, spanning as far back as I can remember in childhood, I thank you for the love and support you showed us through the 3 years of the trial. You showed up for every single one of them and I can't tell you how grateful I am that my dad had a friend like you.

Rodney B – I will never forget you. As the DA for my dad's case, you went above and beyond. You answered all my calls and emails, you considered what I brought to your attention, you handled my meltdowns with grace and you held space for my family and I to make it through the trial. I will forever be grateful to you.

Lorrie R- I can't express my gratitude enough for your support, kindness and perspective. This is not just a token of gratitude for your support during this tragic time, but a recognition of the countless moments, both big and small, where your friendship has been a guiding light. I honor the bond that surpasses the trials of life. Thank you for being a confidant, a rock, and forever my OG desert bestie. Love you.

Jennifer M - The journey of writing this book would not have been the same without your enthusiasm and support. You are forever my "Hype" girl! Thank you for your support during the trial years, for making me laugh and for recommending that I read that book that you said, "You could have written this" which got me off my ass to write my own story. In the midst of shared grief (you losing your mother shortly after I lost my dad) we discovered a unique bond that transcends the tragedies we both endured. I honor not only the shared moments of grief but the laughter and love that echoed through the healing process and continues on.

Wendy A- Your irreplaceable thread of steady support has been a constant presence in my life for over 25 years. This is not just an acknowledgement of your support during challenging times I faced or ones we have faced together, but also a celebration of a friendship that has weathered the many storms of life with grace, love and understanding. Your belief in my abilities, during any facet of life, has had a profound impact on me. I pay homage to the enduring bond that time has only strengthened. Love you.

Cathy F- You are, by far, the best training partner (weight-lifting) I've ever had. I never got back to the person I was when you and I were so dedicated in the gym, prior to my tragedy. Not yet, anyways. I am ever so grateful for your empathy, your care, support, kindness and friendship during my journey. Your compassion and love are so appreciated. I continue to be grateful to call you friend. You are a true gem.

My cousin, Lora and her best friend, John- Our tradition for Thanksgiving is something I cherish and look forward to every year. You both have been an amazing support in all my endeavors, hardships, and triumphs. I love and cherish you both.

Isabel M- I want to express my deepest gratitude for the impact you have had in my life. Your strength and resilience throughout your own grief journey has left me in complete awe. I cherish the friendship and bond we developed along the way, now and always. Love you.

Teri and Stan Hill (Thunder Roads Northern California Magazine)- Thank you for giving me my initial voice to get "My Story" out which I hope raised awareness for our shared commitment of relaying the dangers and the effects of texting and driving/distracted driving. I am forever grateful for that opportunity, as well as, having built the friendship we gained from it.

To the friends not mentioned by name- I would like to extend my heartfelt appreciation to the countless friends who, in your support and understanding, provided solace during times of profound sorrow. While your names may not be specifically mentioned, your collective presence and kindness have been a source of strength, helping me navigate the challenging journey through tragedy, grief and healing. Your unspoken gestures and shared moments have left an indelible mark on my heart, reminding me that, even in the darkest hours, the warmth of true friendship is a guiding light.

To the friendships lost along the way- Though our paths have since diverged, I want to express my sincere gratitude for your willingness to stand by me after the tragedy. You were there for me, at times, when I needed it most. Life may have taken us on different journeys, but the support, as well as the friendship we had over the span of many years, forever remains etched in my heart. I still wish the best for you.

About the Author

Shauna Judnich resides in the Coachella Valley in California. She is a Navy Veteran, outdoor enthusiast, and passionate advocate for healing and self-discovery. With a deep understanding of the complexities of grief and trauma, she embarked on a personal journey of healing and transformation, which ultimately led her to share her experiences in "Echoes of the Soul: Navigating the Path of Grief and Trauma to Healing."

As an Emotion and Body Code practitioner, Shauna brings a holistic approach to healing, combining her personal experiences with her expertise in energy healing modalities. Her dedication to helping others on their healing journey shines through every page of "Echoes of the Soul," offering practical advice, heartfelt anecdotes, and a compassionate understanding of the human experience. When she's not writing, crafting or helping others on their healing journey, you can find Shauna exploring the great outdoors, hiking through various mountains, jet skiing at the river in Arizona, or enjoying quality time with her family.

You can find her often posting inspiration and resonating quotes on TikTok or Instagram under the handle:

@SincerelyShaunaXo
or on her website **www.sincerelyshaunaxo.com**

32542480R00107